D1234485

Leadership Matters...

The CEO Survival Manual

WHAT IT TAKES TO REACH THE C-SUITE

AND STAY THERE

MIKE MYATT

Outskirts Press, Inc.
Denver, Colorado

Leadership Matters...The CEO Survival Manual
What It Takes to Reach the C-Suite and Stay There
All Rights Reserved.
Copyright © 2008 Mike Myatt
V2.0 R 1.2

Cover Photo © 2008 JupiterImages Corporation. All rights reserved - used with permission.

Outskirts Press, Inc.
http://www.outskirtspress.com

ISBN: 978-1-4327-1773-5

Library of Congress Control Number: 2007941378

Outskirts Press and the "OP" logo are trademarks belonging to Outskirts Press, Inc.

PRINTED IN THE UNITED STATES OF AMERICA

Table of Contents

Acknowledgements

I have always said that while I take complete responsibility for all of my failures, I take very little credit for any of my successes. I don't pen these words with a sense of false humility, but rather a simple and sincere recognition that I have been afforded many blessings in life that I could never be so arrogant as to take the credit for.

The previous sentiments clearly apply to this book being published. While it was most certainly my fingers striking the keyboard creating the text that would end up on the following pages, this book was far from a solo effort. The simple truth of the matter is that most people don't say "thank you" often enough and rarely is public recognition given to those who truly deserve it. While I could likely fill several pages with the names of those who contributed to my career or my personal and professional development (some via positive experiences and many through the trials of adversity) I'm going to focus my acknowledgements on those that deserve them the most…my family.

First I'd like to thank my parents, Lew and Myrna Myatt, for having the patience to endure raising me. I feel nothing but gratitude and love toward them for never giving up on me and not strangling me several times over while waiting for me to grow up.

To my wife of 23 years Jane, whose unconditional love and support has carried me, inspired me and taught me many lessons about strength, faith and character. She is the most honest and sincere person I've ever known, the love of my life and a bright light to all who come in contact with her. Jane has always defended me even when I didn't deserve it, and regardless of what is happening in our world at any given time she is always there for me. I love her with all my heart and soul.

To my son Daniel who may have taught me more about being a man than I taught him. A true man of courage, passion, character and commitment that I love, admire and respect more than he will ever know. I couldn't be more proud of him as he displays all the qualities that every father hopes for in a son.

To my daughter Amanda, who knows how to live life to its fullest and can always bring out the best in people. I cherish her as much for her strength and loyalty as I do her compassion and candor. She is brilliant, beautiful, honest, and the one person in this world that can always make me smile. I must also thank her husband Tyler for allowing me to be confident that she'll always be cared for and loved long after I'm gone.

Each of the people mentioned above are not motivated by things or perceptions, and they also exhibit many of the qualities associated with a concept (the difference between success and significance) that we'll discuss in great detail later in the book. My family is a living testament to the old statement that if you look at a man's family you'll learn more about the man than you ever would by looking just at the man alone.

Preface

If you're a current CEO looking to increase the odds of survival and enhance your career longevity, or an aspiring CEO desiring to shave time off your career path then this book was written for you. In addition to having served as a CEO in four of my own ventures as well as having also held that position in the corporate world, much of my working life has been spent as a professional advisor assisting very successful executives and entrepreneurs in managing their careers. I've had both successes and failures (anyone who cannot admit failure is not being honest) and it is the totality of my personal and professional experiences that has given me the insight and perspective to help others. Furthermore it is precisely this combination of experiences that has allowed me to form very solid opinions as to why a cross section of professionals with similar traits and characteristics can have such a wide variance in job performance and tenure.

It is important for you to know that the reason I authored this book wasn't to check-off an item on a list of professional accomplishments, but rather it was to address what I believe is a huge void in the market. While there are many sources available to you on related topics, most of them discuss theory and not practice. The truth is that most of us have read a wide variety of books on the topic of leadership, and we have likely also experienced similar results in that most of these books simply weren't very helpful.

Sure, I'll agree that it can be entertaining, and perhaps even stimulating to debate the benefits and drawbacks of esoteric business theory, however the problem is that those types of discussions don't typically provide you with actionable information. Abstract thinking rarely leads to connecting the dots in a tangible fashion thus restricting the ability to achieve performance gains. Hypothetical discourse by its nature is conducted at such a high level that you will seldom experience any real applicational value as a result of such dialogue. While interesting, the discussions always seem to remain in an ethereal state of theoretical ambiguity. They don't, and can't, function as a guide to action. It is only by drilling down to the atomic level of any subject that true value is achieved. Specificity of thought and conversation shatters the comfort and safety sought by those who prefer to remain in the shadows of vague rhetoric.

What this book is intended to do is to be different…not to provide you with useless rhetoric, but rather to provide you with the information you need as a CEO to create a road map for success. The text that follows is not politically correct, nor is it meant to appease the concerns of anyone who is not a CEO. It is written for the CEO…those that have the toughest and loneliest job on the planet, and who oddly enough have the fewest useful resources available to them. I could have written a much longer book and addressed a much broader cross section of topical content, but my goal was to give you counsel in the areas that I believe will have the most significant impact on your career and your life.

By keeping this book brief it is my hope that you'll not

only read it in its entirety, but that you'll also refer to it over and over again. I urge you to read this book with pen and highlighter in hand so that you can maximize the value of the content contained herein. This book will be a success in my mind if it becomes one of the most dog-eared reference pieces in your personal library...if you have to break out the duct tape because you've worn out the binding then you will have garnered the benefits of what I wanted to communicate.

The simple truth of the matter is that most CEOs fall prey to misunderstanding and/or mismanaging the many constituencies competing for their time and attention. They spend far too much time working on the wrong things for the wrong reasons. It is not at all unusual for CEOs to allow themselves to get dragged down into the weeds where they have little chance of optimizing their performance. Moreover, many chief executives don't really possess a true understanding of their job description to begin with, and of those that do, many cannot adapt to perform as needed based upon unique or changing contextual, situational or environmental scenarios.

As I alluded to above, the counsel put forth between the covers of this book is not based on academic theory, but on 25+ years of in the trenches, real world experience. I'll provide you with actionable advice that will allow you to lift yourself above the noise and see things with a new sense of clarity and a renewed perspective on what really matters.

It is my fondest hope that reading this book will prove to be one of the most valuable investments you have made in yourself, your career and your family. It is not only chalk-full of battle tested, practical advice that will help you refine your professional game, but it will also help you understand how to reach the heights of corporate success without sacrificing your family or your values ...

Chapter 1

Introduction...A Little Perspective on What Really Matters

"A life absent self examination is not worth living"
– Plato

While there is plenty of *"CEO centric"* advice in the chapters that follow, it would be nothing short of tragic if I didn't address the bigger picture right from the outset as a foundation for readers to build upon. I have the benefit of not only having a few grey hairs myself (I guess I should be thankful that I still have hair), but I have also had the privilege of working with many executives and professionals as they near the end of their careers.

Having the advantage of hindsight I can say with great certainty that who you are as a person is infinitely more important than the job you hold. There are few things in life as thought provoking as witnessing what by all outward appearances seems to be a successful executive, but as you begin to peel back the layers of their carefully crafted

1

veneer you quickly come to realize that they are little more than an empty, bitter and frustrated person. These are the individuals who confuse career accomplishments with life accomplishments. They work their entire career chasing some illusive form of fulfillment only to fade into the sunset with nothing more than an empty lifetime of regrets as their reward.

If someone asks you to tell them about yourself and you proceed to tell them what your job is then we have some work to do...You see there is nothing but downside associated with being defined by what you do. If you allow this to happen you will always end-up selling yourself short for your worth is far greater than any title that can be printed on a business card. If you define yourself by what you do as opposed to the entirety of who you are it is more likely than not that you will suffer from at least some if not all of the following six problematic symptoms:

1. You are a workaholic;
2. You have a social deficit;
3. Your stress level is off the charts;
4. You're are not the most pleasant person to be around;
5. You have relationship issues, and;
6. Your physical health is not what it should be.

The good news is that it doesn't have to be this way. You can make the choice right now to live your life with your integrity, your family, your health and your friends intact, or you can sacrifice those things to bolster your professional ego. I have witnessed the inevitable sadness and despair that occurs when an executive places his or her career above all things to the extent that it defines who they are. Conversely I've observed the satisfaction and happiness that can be achieved when executives have balance and perspective such that work is what they do, but clearly not who they are. Do not allow yourself to be defined by your title, but rather strive to be defined by the totality of your life's work. You can certainly make great professional contributions along the way, but the emphasis of your life's work should clearly be placed on your contributions to family, friends and society. Don't succumb to moral relativism where everything is rationalized or justified as nothing more than a means to and end, rather let your values drive your vision.

I've personally known far too many executives who have successfully achieved a work/life balance to listen to the meaningless drivel of those that say you cannot have it all. While it makes for a great sound bite to appease those who have made poor choices, to say that in order to be a successful CEO your career has to come first it is really little more than a pathetic excuse. Your career clearly needs to be *a* priority, but certainly not *the* priority. The truth of the matter is that all your stakeholders would prefer you have balance, health, perspective and personal fulfillment, because you'll simply be more effective on the job, not to mention more pleasant to be around.

When coaching and mentoring CEOs one of my biggest challenges with most clients is having them align what's truly important to them with how they actually live their lives. I'm always amazed at the number of otherwise savvy executives who have their careers mapped out down to the most minute detail, but have no plan whatsoever with regard to having a successful life. It's as if they believe that if they're successful enough at work they'll have the economic freedom such that everything else will just fall into place. Wouldn't it be nice if it were that easy? Regrettably life doesn't work that way...

Attitude, performance, philanthropic interests, balance between work and family life, physical health and many other critically important things that lead to success and happiness often come down to nothing more than being honest with yourself about why you do what you do. Do yourself a favor and pause right now to perform what is likely a long overdue gut check by answering the following questions:

1. How do you define success? Moreover how does your family define success? How large does your paycheck or net worth really have to be? How much is really enough? Are you focused on the right things for the right reasons?

2. How do your friends, family and coworkers feel about you? How do you feel about you? What do you see when you look in the mirror? Given where you are in life have you accomplished what you had hoped to accomplish by this point in time?

3. When you wake-up in the morning do you feel excited about the day ahead, or do you feel frustrated, anxious, or overwhelmed not even wanting to get out of bed? Are you happy, balanced, satisfied, fulfilled and content? If not, why not? Do you know what actions to take to close the gap between where you are and where you want to be? What can you do **NOW** to begin making changes?

4. Most professionals operate according to a business plan, but few have a life plan. Do you have a written life plan? Is your business plan aligned with your life plan? Are your daily actions in alignment with achieving the goals

contained in your plans? Do you live according to your values and/or your faith or do you easily compromise them when convenient?

5. If you were hit by a truck tomorrow how much unfinished business would be left behind? Have you said the things you need to say to your friends and loved ones? What legacy would you leave behind and would you feel good about it or disturbed by it?

6. When was the last time you told someone that you loved, respected or admired them? When was the last time you sacrificed something for the greater good and benefit of others?

Okay, it goes without saying that the list of aforementioned questions could certainly be expanded, and I would actually encourage you to do so solely based upon what's important to you and those you care about. It is this type of critical thinking exercise that should determine how you shape your career objectives. To use a bit of *"CEO Speak"* it is your personal KPIs (Key Performance Indicators) that should be used to reverse engineer your career planning process and not the other way around as is typical with most executives.

Listen, I'm not so naïve in my approach that I believe the philosophy being espoused in this chapter will be easy to implement. I realize that if you have chosen to be a CEO you'll find it much more difficult to bifurcate your career from the rest of you life. When you sign-up for a senior leadership role it comes with high expectations and numerous responsibilities which make it difficult (if not impossible) to just throw the switch into the off position and walk out the door at 5:00pm leaving your work behind. In fact, entrepreneurs and executives with this mentality are likely to be very frustrated individuals who don't live-up to their own expectations or those of others. As I said above, I'm not saying it's easy, but I am clearly saying that it is very doable if you have your priorities in order. As a CEO you're going to put in more than a 40 hour week, but it can be on your terms by design and not on the terms of others by default. Remember that it is perfectly okay for your career to be *a* priority, so long as it does not become *the* priority.

If you are a CEO and you feel ambivalent, frustrated, unmotivated or trapped in your career, it is likely because what you do is not in sync with who you are, or the things that are truly important to you. For passion in the workplace to be anything more than a fleeting state of mind you must align your personal values, goals and interests with what you do for a living. I'm not suggesting that you define who you are by what you do, rather I'm suggesting that if what you do is in balance with your priorities and interests you'll be able to remain productive and passionate about what you do over the long haul.

I have always believed that those CEOs who have a handle on work/life balance can sustain a sense of passion throughout their careers. As a result their careers are nothing short of a marvelous adventure as opposed to being relegated to the drudgery of a day-to-day grind. The best part is they can partake in the great adventure without making unnecessary sacrifices that will be regretted down the road.

The bottom line is that you have to want this more than I want you to want this...It is your choice to make and yours alone. All I ask is that you take the time to consider what I've outlined in this chapter and I offer you my best wishes for making a wise choice...

Chapter 2

CEO...The Toughest Job on the Org Chart

UNDERSTANDING YOUR JOB DESCRIPTION AS CEO-

"A leader is one who knows the way, goes the way and shows the way."

- John Maxwell

S o, you want to be a CEO? Well you're not alone...the reality is that most executives have thought about it at some point in time even if only to second guess their boss. As with most things in life thinking about something as contrasted with actually doing something are altogether quite different propositions.

Let's begin with taking a look at the numbers...only about 1/1000 of 1% of the total worldwide workforce will ever become a CEO. Even if you're good enough to reach the corner office you should know that the average tenure of a CEO has fallen to an all time low of just less than 4 years. Furthermore out of those who defy the odds and become the chief executive more than half of them will be regarded as failures. Of those CEOs that succeed, only a small percentage will be regarded as truly great CEOs.

What existing CEOs know that aspiring CEOs have not yet figured out is that there is no tougher job than that of the Chief Executive Officer. Let me be very clear...if you think you want to be a CEO so that you can kick back and put your feet up on the desk while barking out orders and raking in the big bucks, STOP HERE...put this book aside now because you are not CEO material...you are delusional.

No single position within the corporate hierarchy receives the unrelenting and often terse scrutiny (public and private) that a CEO must deal with. The pressure is intense and the risks are high, but the rewards can be tremendous for those who possess the requisite leadership skills and character to hold the title of chief executive. Many CEOs initially rise to their position based upon leveraging a particular skill set, however a single area of strength will rarely be enough to keep a CEO in the corner office for long. Those CEOs who remain in the position long-term do so largely based upon the ability to broaden and deepen their skill sets and competencies while developing a clear understanding for the priorities of the job.

So, let's assume for a moment that you're the CEO...You've worked long and hard to climb the corporate ladder, or you bet the family farm and took the entrepreneurial risk of starting your own enterprise...either way, you're intelligent, passionate, committed, experienced and ready to lead your company onward and upward. Whether self-appointed or bestowed upon you, now that your business card reads CEO how do you really measure-up? Let's look beyond the title and see what it takes to become a truly great CEO...

It is true that the proverbial buck stops with the CEO, and that the CEO is ultimately responsible for the success or failure of a company. The final responsibility for operations, strategy, finance, branding, advertising, PR, marketing, corporate culture, HR, compliance, sales, etc. all rest with the CEO. Therein lies the conundrum for most Chief Executives...While one person clearly cannot do it all, the CEO also cannot abdicate responsibility. On one end of the spectrum many CEOs either misunderstand the difference between ultimate responsibility and day-to-day responsibility, or on the other end of the spectrum they cannot or will not accept responsibility for anything. The truly great CEOs clearly understand their role within the enterprise, become excellent leaders and are masters of execution. They realize the influence they possess and the powerful impact that their decisions and actions have both internally and externally. They neither take on too much responsibility nor do they ignore their responsibility...

We've all witnessed the CEO who tries to do too much, and conversely most of us have also observed the chief executive in stealth mode who accomplishes very little. We've gladly followed the bright, affable and charismatic CEOs and rebelled against the arrogant and self indulgent chief executives who love to do little more than pontificate about their legendary prowess. So what makes a great CEO? The answer to this question will be addressed in great detail throughout this book, but for now suffice it to say that the answer is complex. Great CEOs possess many individual qualities that have been refined over time to a level of sophistication and savvy that allows them to consistently function at very high levels.

Believe it or not, the biggest challenge a CEO faces is gaining a true understanding of their job description...The fact of the matter is that a CEO is responsible for everything…yes I mean everything. Because the CEO is ultimately held accountable for the success or failure of the company, he/she must assume responsibility for enterprise wide performance. Therein lies the great mystery surrounding the position of CEO…How can they possibly do it all? The reality is that they can't, but you'd be surprised at how many try…

They key to becoming a great CEO is to understand the differences between duties and responsibilities. The CEO's duties are the activities he/or she actually performs, or in other words, the responsibilities that don't get delegated to others. While the CEO clearly cannot endeavor to be all things to all people while attempting to do everything on his/her own, the CEO must lock onto and own certain mission critical duties. Not everything can or should be delegated…In the text that follows I'll put forth the areas which the CEO must view as his/her duties to own, perform and master:

Become a True Leader: Respect is a trait that can rarely be commanded for any sustainable period of time, but rather respect is at its best and strongest when it has been earned. It is not only through success that confidence is instilled, but also in doing things properly regardless of the outcome. Management and staff will work through failures alongside leaders that possess integrity and character, and by contrast, will resent and mock the success of those leaders who prosper due to ill-gotten gains. In addition to being productive and effective, great leaders understand the inherent value found in remaining approachable and human. Communication and conflict resolution skills need to be developed to their maximum. We'll delve into this topic in much greater detail in chapter two…

Set the Tone: Successful CEOs set the tone for the company. A truly great CEO understands that his/her primary role is to create the corporate vision and mission and use those to determine the appropriate corporate strategy. Don't get caught up in attempting to develop something catchy for the purpose of being encapsulated within a piece of framed artwork that hangs in your reception area, but yet is never put into practice. It is much more important that your vision and mission be understood by company employees and translated into the resultant authenticity of their actions. Your customers don't care what you put on paper, but they care immensely about whether or not a company's vision and mission are reflected in a fulfilled brand promise.

I developed a simple organizational framework several years ago which defines the order of operations surrounding management theory. It has been widely adopted by business schools and corporations alike and will serve as a useful backdrop to how successful CEOs create a powerful business model. It goes like this..."*Vision* dictates *Mission* which determines *Strategy*, which surfaces *Goals* that frame *Objectives*, which in turn drives the *Tactics* that tell an organization what *Resources*, *Infrastructure* and *Processes* are needed to support a certainty of execution" (Mike Myatt, 1988).

Great CEOs realize that few things are as important as unifying resources and actions with opportunities. Strategic decisioning must be aligned with vision and mission. It is the clarity of the CEO's vision that instills purpose, which in turn creates the passion that will drive focus and productivity. These traits will create a positive culture which is crucial for long-term success. Each and every action or inaction on the part of the CEO makes a cultural statement. Because the work of the corporation is performed by people and people are profoundly impacted by culture, the CEO must insure a healthy, safe and positive culture.

Great CEOs set the tone for corporate culture from the top-down. Successful Chief Executives do not allow culture to evolve by default over time, rather they engineer culture by design to support and foster an environment which will enable sustainable success. Great CEOs realize that it takes top talent to create successful companies, and absent the right corporate culture you cannot attract or retain top talent. Great CEOs heavily influence culture...Everything from how they dress, to what they say and who they say it to, to the positions they adopt as well as to the company they keep make a very visible statement by which they will be judged and held accountable.

The key to creating a successful culture as a CEO is to not see yourself as the supreme authority at the top of a hierarchical organizational chart, but rather to view yourself as the catalyst at the center of the organization. CEOs that establish high functioning cultures that accomplish great things do so not by means of outdated and insecure management practices that function through authoritative command and control tactics, but rather by serving, enabling, mentoring and leading their workforce.

Focus on Team Building: A CEO that abdicates control of player personnel is taking on huge amounts of risk. The CEO must take responsibility for recruiting, deploying, mentoring and retaining the executive team. The executive team will in turn lead and manage the balance of the organization. An alignment of vision, mission and strategy between the CEO and the executive team is crucial for creating a healthy and sustainable enterprise. If the executive team is not functioning smoothly this is a reflection of poor leadership and team building skills on the part of the CEO.

Great CEOs focus on team building. They not only know how to attract and motivate top talent, but they

12

understand how to deploy the talent in the most meaningful fashion by applying the best talent to the most significant opportunities. Great CEOs understand that they cannot do everything and therefore do everything possible to surround themselves with the best executive team possible. Great companies are focused, collaborative and innovative which only happens in an organization created and/or led by great CEOs.

Understand Resource Allocation: As mentioned above, great CEOs insure that the best talent is applied toward the best opportunities. Moreover the CEO needs to insure that the proper financial and non-financial resources are applied appropriately across the enterprise. While not all CEOs possess strong finance backgrounds, they are still ultimately responsible for the financial decisions that can determine the company's fate.

Jack Welch the former head of GE built a reputation as one of the great business leaders of this era. When asked how he transformed a lack-luster, institutional, global corporate giant into a dynamic culture focused on innovation and growth, Welch responded by saying; "My job is to put the best people on the biggest opportunities and the best allocation of dollars in the right places. That's about it. Transfer ideas, allocate resources and get out of the way." Welch clearly not only understood the concept of organizational leverage through proper deployment of talent and resources...He mastered it.

Become the brand champion: Since there is an entire chapter of this book dedicated to branding I'm not going to spend much time addressing the subject here other than to say that great CEOs make branding a priority. A good CEO is the public face of the company. CEOs need to not only champion the brand internally but also evangelize the brand externally. CEOs that don't heavily promote the company brand throughout the entire value chain are not doing their job. If the CEO is not intimately familiar with what it takes to increase brand equity then it is only a matter of time until the company will see a brand in decline.

Bottom line...As a CEO your ultimate success or failure will be directly tied to the growth and sustainability of your corporate and personal brand equity. As such your company's brand guardian should be the brand owner (you as the CEO) and not your ad agency or PR firm.

As I mentioned at the beginning of this chapter, a CEO's job is rather simple but not easy...You don't have to do all things, rather just focus on the right priorities with the proper talent and resources and your enterprise will prosper.

NAVIGATING THE MINEFIELD – THE VIEW FROM THE TOP ISN'T ALWAYS BETTER...

"If the blind lead the blind, both will fall in the ditch"
- The Bible (Matthew 15:14)

Now that you understand the basics of the job description, let's examine how to avoid becoming a CEO who is destined to fail. How many times have you watched a CEO give a favorable assessment of expected company performance to the board of directors, the bank, shareholders, analysts, employees or the media only to be proven woefully incorrect? I'm always amazed at the number of CEOs who are out of touch with the operating realities of their company. In this next section I'll share my thoughts on what you don't want to become as a CEO and why the view isn't always better from the top...

So the question is how does a CEO get to the point of

being so disconnected from operations that he or she just doesn't have a clue? The reality is that there are any number of reasons why this can happen, and these reasons are best understood by identifying the characteristics of CEOs most likely to fail as noted below:

The Overly Optimistic CEO: I have met many CEOs over the years that simply choose to view the world through rose colored glasses. They will believe what they want to believe regardless of what they hear or see. Even in the worst of times they believe nothing to be insurmountable. While overly optimistic CEOs are usually great corporate cheerleaders, they are a far cry from being realists. Often times the overly optimistic CEO will suffer significant losses in credibility due to recurring problems in reconciling fact from fiction.

While I'm certainly not advocating becoming a pessimist, as a CEO it is crucial that you develop the ability to maintain an optimistic outlook balanced by intellect and reason. Not understanding the differences between unattainable hurdles and achievable objectives will set-up both you and your business for failure. Everyone reading this book has likely observed a CEO who was guilty of wanting something to be true so badly that they disregarded several warning signs on the way to crashing and burning...

I counsel every one of my clients to ask "how realistic is it that we can accomplish this" for any recommendation they receive, and then I further encourage them to critically validate the response. As a CEO you get paid for putting points on the scoreboard not for pursuing initiatives destined for failure. Overly optimistic CEO's tend to think of everyone as their friend and will take any report or piece of information at face value. These CEOs are far too trusting and politically naive. They fail to seek clarification, validation, or proof supporting the information they have been fed. The overly optimistic CEO is usually their own worst enemy becoming the eventual cause of their own undoing.

The Arrogant CEO: These are the schizophrenic CEOs who combine the traits of overly optimistic CEOs with an overarching attitude of self importance…The arrogant CEO believes they can will their view into reality in spite of circumstances, situations or events. The arrogant CEO doesn't value the input of line and staff management. These CEOs see management opinions as inconsequential, unless of course they happen to be in alignment with their own opinion. Arrogant CEOs quickly alienate their workforce by unwittingly converting potential allies into adversaries. A CEO who lacks the ability to create a trust bond and engender loyalty and confidence from their employees will be a CEO destined to fail.

Confidence vs. Arrogance…is it merely a question of semantics? I think not…While confidence can be mistaken for arrogance and vice versa, they are clearly not interchangeable terms. There is great power that resides within the truly confident CEO as contrasted with self-destructive characteristics that plague the arrogant CEO. In the competitive world of business a reserved attitude of humility can often be misinterpreted as a sign of weakness. However if you've ever negotiated with a truly confident and humble person you'll find that their resolve is much greater than the feigned confidence of the arrogant. Confident CEOs are unflappable professionals who can remain calm, cool and collected regardless of the situation at hand, while arrogant CEOs are turbulent individuals whose tirades are often legendary.

The truth of the matter is that few things have inspired and motivated me over the years like the quiet confidence and humility of great leaders. I would much rather listen to the self-deprecating humor of a confident person making fun of themselves than the mean spirited attacks of an arrogant person waged at someone else's expense. More importantly, I would much rather work for or along side the understated than the overstated. Those CEOs who demonstrate a true respect for others regardless of their station in life are much more likely to be successful over the long-term than those that use the tactics of disrespect to humiliate and intimidate.

While arrogant people can and often do succeed in business, I believe that it comes at a great personal and professional cost. Arrogance rarely results in lasting relationships built on a foundation of loyalty and trust. Rather arrogant people typically find themselves surrounded by exploitive individuals who are all to happy to ride the "gravy-train" in good times, but at the first sign of trouble all you will see is their backs as they run for the hills. The confident also succeed in business, but not at the expense of others as do the arrogant. You'll find confident leaders have broader spheres of influence, attract better talent, engender more confidence, and earn more loyalty and respect than do those that lead with solely with bravado.

If what you're seeking is lasting relationships, long-term success and a better quality of life (in and out of the workplace) then you will be better served to forego the pompous acts of the arrogant for the humility and quiet confidence displayed by true leaders.

The Multitasking CEO: One of the most common problems facing CEOs is the lack of ability to remain focused on highest and best use activities. In fact many executives are their own worst enemy when it comes to taking themselves out of the "productivity zone". While we could talk about being better managers of technology, communications, interruptions and various other productivity killers, there are many other books that address those issues. Therefore I will focus on the number one killer of CEO productivity which is biting-off more than you can chew or what I like to call *initiative overload...*

Fact: bright, talented CEOs with a bias to action will often take on more than they should. Fiction: multitasking accomplishes more than focused effort. The reality is that maximizing results and creating a certainty of execution is all about focus, focus and more focus...A CEO can only act in the here and now, so the knowledge and skill required to master any endeavor only happens when they focus on what they're doing. This is the definition of presence and it is only when CEOs operate in the present that high performance, disruptive innovation and fluidity occur.

Is your rubber-band stretched so tight that it's about to snap? Efficiency and productivity are not found working at or even near capacity. Rather entering the productivity zone is found working at about 60% to 80% of capacity. Operating in excess of that threshold will cause increased stress, lack of attention to detail and errant decisioning. In fact, if you can consistently operate in a productive capacity more than 50% of the time you'll find yourself in the top 10% of all executives with regard to performance.

It is important for CEOs to learn to apply focused leverage to a limited number of highest and best use activities rather than to continually shift gears between multiple initiatives. Resist the temptation to just advance a broad number of disparate initiatives and alternatively focus your efforts on the completion of a few high impact objectives. The simple reality is that if you continue to add new responsibilities to an already full plate, all of your obligations will suffer as a result. Face current challenges head-on by keeping your head down and applying focused leverage to the task at hand.

Don't delude yourself into thinking that changing direction mid-stream will produce better results as it rarely will. Remember that most people who fail just quit a bit too early in the process. While I'm certainly not recommending blind faith that flies in the face of solid business logic, neither am I encouraging you to run away by changing focus or tactics when the right thing to do is stay the course regardless of the difficulties that may present themselves.

It is through the accomplishment of current objectives that the victories are won and success is born. The achievement of current goals and objectives free up the time and create the resources to move on to bigger and better things...Trying to do too many things at once will impede progress, dilute effort and energy, add to chaos and lead to burn-out. Bottom line...success equals focus.

The Polarizing CEO: These are the CEOs who unwittingly pit various constituencies against one another because they can't make decisions on their own. While they are sometimes referred to as consensus builders, I feel this is far too polite a term that legitimizes a very destructive practice. The polarizing CEOs are neither a micro-manager nor do they understand delegation. These CEO's tend to be disconnected simply because they have a difficult time forming their own opinions. In fact, I refer to them as opinion shoppers...they wander hither and yon shopping for opinions and as a result end-up polarizing people by having them work against one another instead of with one another. These CEOs display a fundamental lack of leadership and team building skills.

It is almost as if the polarizing CEO feels that if they

19

have enough different people working on the same program that certainly someone will eventually succeed. These CEOs while not completely unengaged, are a far cry from being productively engaged... I have a VC friend who refers to this phenomenon as the sea-gull theory of management: "They fly in, flap their wings, make a lot of noise, crap all over everything and fly back out again." Don't get me wrong, I believe a wise CEO seeks the input and counsel of others during the decisioning process. However, it simply boils down to the fact that great CEOs know the difference between collaborative leadership and management by consensus.

The Disconnected CEO: Unlike CEOs who understand how to leverage time and resources via delegation while remaining connected to management and staff the disconnected CEO does just the opposite. They have reclusive tendencies which cause them to often completely abdicate responsibility and remain disconnected from management by sequestering themselves in the corner office. These are the "closed door" operators who create a maze of barriers and obstacles between themselves and others making it difficult to ever gain access to them. Operating in a vacuum and being out of touch is never a good position to find yourself in as the CEO. I have consistently espoused the value of walking the floor, dropping in on meetings on an impromptu basis, taking employees of all ranks to lunch and any number of other items that focus on raising your internal awareness. It is imperative that CEOs understand the value of raising both their internal and external awareness...

My advice to CEOs regardless of whether you're running a start-up or a Fortune 500 company is to go see things for yourself. I think you'll find that your view of the world will change dramatically when you rely upon your own observations as opposed to what your executive dashboard indicates, what you read in a management report or what you hear third or fourth hand in a meeting. Think about it...when you're being interviewed by the media, sitting in front of the board, on an analyst call, speaking at the annual shareholder meeting or interfacing with key customers or suppliers, wouldn't it be great to actually know what your talking about as opposed to interpreting what someone else has told you?

If you're a CEO and you haven't personally spoken with your top customers, suppliers, vendors and partners you're doing yourself and your company a great injustice. If your CFO handles all communications with your banking relationships and your Chief Investment Officer handles all of your investor relations you're flat out missing the boat. If your CMO is making all of your brand decisions there will be h*ll to pay down the road. Moreover in today's litigious and compliance oriented world where the CEO is no longer out of reach its just plain smart to take a more hands on approach. Remember that there is a major difference between delegating and abdicating responsibility.

Let me be very clear...I'm not suggesting that you become a micro manager or that you stop delegating, I'm simply suggesting that you do the job the way it is supposed to be done. Great leaders champion from the front...they are not disengaged invisible executives. As the CEO you are the visionary, influencer, champion, defender, evangelist and you must have a bias to action. You can be none of these things as a recluse...If you want to extend your shelf-life or make yourself more marketable for better opportunities down the road I suggest you be very visible and very active. In addition to leading your organization pay close attention to managing your reputation and your personal brand both inside and outside the company.

The Inappropriately Impassioned CEO: While I have always been a champion of passion as a key success metric, I have recently witnessed a few instances of passion impeding purpose, which in turn hinders success. As I have observed this situation on more than a few occasions over the years, it has been my experience that passion only becomes a barrier to success when it is misunderstood and/or misapplied. Therefore I thought it might be of value to examine the downside of unbridled passion, so that passion can remain an asset and not end-up becoming a liability for you or your company....

Passion is an emotion of exuberance that can almost single-handedly fuel greatness. History is littered with accounts of marginally talented individuals who have risen to greatness based upon little more than being passionate about the pursuit of their objective. Passion creates a "refuse to lose" mentality which can enable the average person to move outside comfort zones, take-on greater risk, go the extra mile and achieve phenomenal results. That being said, passion without perspective and reason can actually serve to distort one's perception of reality allowing them to slip into very dangerous territory. Have you ever known someone who wanted something to be true so badly that they started to adopt positions and manufacture circumstances to support their own false reality? Just because you can convince yourself that your position is correct, doesn't necessarily mean that it is...

Just as there exists a very fine line between brilliance and insanity, there also exists a fine line between passion and many negative traits such as narrow-mindedness, narcissism, fanaticism, delusion and even paranoia. For instance, there is a big difference in an entrepreneur who is passionate about his business and one that is emotionally over-invested in his business. Healthy passion for one's business actually brings focus and clarity of thought which serve to accelerate growth and create sustainable success. However being emotionally over-invested in one's business can lead to irrational decisioning, prideful or ego-driven actions, the use of flawed business logic and poor execution, which can in turn lead to unnecessary loss and/or failure.

It is not at all uncommon for entrepreneurs and executives to be too close to the forest to see the trees. Passionate CEOs thinking clearly will seek independent outside counsel and advice to continually gut-check and refine their thinking. The inappropriately impassioned CEOs will either avoid counsel or surround themselves with the proverbial yes-men. Another trait of healthy passionate thinking is to recruit tier-one talent at the executive leadership and senior management levels in order to stimulate innovation and thought growth. Effective leadership teams have a balance of left-brain and right-brain thinkers from a variety of backgrounds so that they can draw from the broadest possible array of experiences when formulating positions and options. Emotionally over-invested CEOs tend to surround themselves with very small teams of like minded individuals from similar backgrounds who tend to reinforce one another's thinking instead of challenging it.

I applaud those of you reading this text who constitute the passionate minority...I would however also counsel you to take pause and evaluate your current positioning and thinking. Are you operating in a vacuum? Do you seek advice and counsel from those who will tell you the truth or from those who will just tell you what you want to hear? Is your passion creating clarity, focus and purpose or is it blinding you from seeing the reality of your current situation?

If you're a CEO with clouded vision and desire to change the view from the top it is critical that you maintain open lines of communication through a variety of channels and feedback loops. You must maintain a connection and rapport with both line and staff. Furthermore you must refine your intuitive senses. A good CEO demands accountability and transparency. They challenge everything of consequence as gross optimism, general statements, hidden agendas or ambiguity and see these things as only contributing to blind spots and limiting vision...

BECOMING A GREAT CEO

"Risk more than others think safe, dream more than others think practical, expect more than others think possible and care more than others think wise."
- Howard Schultz, Chairman, Starbucks

Okay, we've covered the job description of a CEO and the common mistakes to avoid as a CEO, so now I'll give you a sneak-peak at what lies ahead in the forthcoming chapters by providing an overview of what it takes to become a great CEO. The harsh reality is that becoming a great CEO becomes more difficult with each passing year. I can remember a time in the not too distant past when little more than a combination of putting in your time and not making any huge mistakes was often enough to propel you to the C-suite...those days have long sense passed.

The rapidly changing global landscape and the evolving complexity of business makes the job of CEO something that is only well suited for a rare few. As we've already seen it takes a gifted, motivated and multi-disciplined individual to survive the pressure and challenges that chief executives are faced with. For these reasons sustainable success at the C-suite level is an elusive thing in today's business world. It is critical for executives to understand what it takes to beat the odds and so the balance of this chapter will provide you with an overview of the characteristics that a CEO must posses in order to maintain his or her position and remain in control for as long as they choose...

A major part of the job description for a CEO deals with managing expectations. Put simply a CEO's shelf life will be equal to their ability to align vision with execution in a manner that is congruous to the expectations of key constituencies. A CEO must be able to focus on deploying the necessary resources at the right time to achieve the desired results. By exhibiting strong leadership skills a good CEO will manage talent, performance, change, innovation, influence, rapport, and messaging to consistently drive an enterprise forward regardless of circumstances. If you want to insure longevity as a CEO work towards a mastery of the following characteristics (all of which will be covered in greater detail in subsequent chapters):

1. **Integrity**: Always do the right thing regardless of sentiment and never compromise your core values. If you cannot build trust and engender confidence with your stakeholders you cannot succeed. No amount of talent can overcome illegal, immoral or otherwise ill-advised actions. A leader void of integrity will not survive over the long-haul.

2. **Excellent Decision Making Skills**: As a CEO you will live or die by the quality of the decisions you make. When you're the CEO good decisioning is expected, poor decisioning won't be tolerated and great decisioning will

set you apart from the masses.

3. **Ability to Focus**: If you cannot focus you cannot perform at the level necessary to remain in the C-suite for very long. The ability to do nothing more than understand and lock onto priorities will place you in the top 10% of all executives.

4. **Leveraging Experience**: Inexperience, a lack of maturity, needing to be the center of attention, not recognizing limitations, a lack of judgment, an inferior knowledge base or any number of other common mistakes made by rookie CEOs can cause your house of cards to fall. If you don't possess the experience personally, hire it, contract it, but by all means acquire it. Great CEOs surround themselves with tier-one talent and the best advisors money can buy. They don't make uninformed or ill-advised decisions in a vacuum.

5. **Command Presence**: Great CEOs possess a strong presence and bearing. They are unflappable individuals that never let you see them sweat (unless of course it serves a purpose). Everything from how they carry themselves to how they speak and dress messages that they are in charge.

6. **Embracing Change**: Great CEOs have a strong bias to action. They don't rest upon past accomplishments and are always seeking to improve through change and innovation. In today's fast paced and competitive environment those CEOs who don't openly embrace change will often be shown the door prior to the expiration of their initial employment contract.

7. **Brand Champions**: Great CEOs understand branding at every level. They seek to build not only a dominant corporate brand, but also a strong personal brand. CEOs that are not well branded on a personal basis or who let their corporate brand fall into decline will not survive.

8. **Boundless Energy**: Great CEOs have a boundless

amount of energy. They are positive in their outlook and their attitude is contagious. A low energy CEO is not motivating, convincing or credible.

9. **Business Acumen**: Great CEOs have a deep understanding of business and a strong orientation toward profit. Great CEOs possess what often appears to be a sixth sense or an almost instinctive feel for what the company needs to do to make money and remain competitive.

10. **People Acumen**: Great CEOs have a nose for talent...They understand how to recruit, develop and deploy talent focusing on applying the best talent to the best opportunities. They also know when it's time to make changes and cut losses as needed.

11. **Organizational Acumen**: Great CEOs know how to engender trust, when and how to share information and are expert listeners. They develop strong and positive corporate cultures driven to performance by aligned motivations. They can quickly diagnose whether the organization is performing at full potential, delivering on commitments and whether the company is changing and growing versus just operating.

12. **Curiosity**: Great CEOs possess a powerful motivation to increase their knowledge base and to convert their learning into actionable initiatives. They question, challenge, confront and are never accepting of the status quo.

13. **Intellectual Capacity**: Great CEOs are also great thinkers both at the strategic and tactical levels. They are quick on their feet and know how to get to the root of an issue faster than anyone else. I've never met a great CEO who wasn't extremely discerning.

14. **Global Mindset**: Regardless of the geographical boundaries of the current business model great CEOs think globally. Limited thinking results in limited results.

Whether global thinking is applied to capital formation, supply-chain issues, business development, strategic partnering, distribution or any number of other areas those CEOs who don't grasp the importance of thinking globally will not endure. Great CEOs are externally oriented, hungry for knowledge of the world and adept at connecting new trends and developments through pattern recognition and being opportunistically focused.

15. **Never Quit**: Great CEOs refuse to lose...It's easier than you might think, just don't quit. Strip away the excuses, rationalizations and justifications and the only thing standing between you and whatever your objective may be is what you see staring back at you when you look in the mirror each morning. Great CEOs have an insatiable appetite for accomplishment and results and while they may reengineer or change direction they will never lose sight of the end game.

Bottom line... You cannot be a successful CEO as a one trick pony. A lack of ability to excel in any one of the aforementioned 15 areas will endanger your chances of success as a chief executive. Successful CEOs recognize their strengths and weaknesses and focus on developing the skill sets and core competencies needed to get the job done.

Chapter 3

Becoming a True Leader...Do You Have What It Takes?

"Having the capacity to lead is not enough. The leader must be willing to use it."

- Vince Lombardi

L et's start this chapter by addressing the first thing you must do to become a great leader which is to get in the game. You cannot accomplish anything by standing on the sidelines waiting for someone else to take action. Leadership is not a spectator sport and great leaders lead from the front by example. They establish rapport and build a trust bond with those they lead. They are present, visible and they always show up for the game.

You cannot survive as a CEO without being anything other than an outstanding leader. Just relying on management skills alone will not work if you intend to be CEO as you must demonstrate the ability to be an effective leader. So before we go any further let's examine the difference between leaders and managers. There has been a tremendous amount of politically correct pontificating of late in corporate circles about the differences between managers and leaders. Most of the commentary I have read attempts to please both audiences. Those of you who have read my work in the past know that I am rarely politically correct (there is a big difference between being politically correct and politically astute), nor do I ever seek to try and please all the people all the time.

There is clearly a need for both managers and leaders in the business world as a solid company is built by properly deploying and utilizing both skill sets. While I respect and have developed close friendships with many a manager, this author simply believes that the law of scarcity applies to the topic at hand. There is an infinitely greater supply of managers causing a much greater demand for leaders. Put simply, because leaders are much more difficult to come by, they are therefore more valuable to an enterprise.

The paragraph above begs the question why are there fewer leaders than managers? I believe the question is answered very easily in the two points made below:

1. Not everyone has it in them to be a leader and thus the old axiom "a born leader". The intrinsic quality of leadership often begins with nothing more than raw talent and a certain state of mind. To possess the innate qualities of a leader is however not the same thing as being a leader. As important as your DNA is, effective leadership skills are developed and refined by time, experience, and a true desire to be more than just a manager, but a true leader.

2. As I mentioned above, not everyone (even those that have the ability) wants to be a leader. As the old saying goes "to whom much is given, much is expected." The reality is that most people would rather have the buck stop with someone else and just fly beneath the radar screen. I

have met several managers who could be great leaders, but choose not to...if they made the choice to rise-up and display their leadership ability they would also quickly rise above the rank and file. The truth is very few individuals are willing to step-up to the plate and accept the many burdens of leadership.

Let's breakdown the DNA of a typical leader...Leaders tend to be very creative, dynamic, outgoing and unflappable individuals. They tend to think big picture focusing on vision and strategy while looking to make a long-term impact. By way of contrast let's examine the DNA of a manager. Managers are usually more analytical while focusing on process and procedure looking to make short-term contributions. The following list adapted from Mind of a Manager, Soul of a Leader by Craig Hickman demonstrates the DNA gap between leaders and managers:

- Managers build systems and procedures, Leaders build teams and develop talent.
- Managers surround themselves with subordinates & Leaders surround themselves with the best & brightest.
- Managers avoid risk and where they can't avoid it they manage it at all costs while Leaders thrive on risk while seeking to leverage and exploit the opportunities associated with risk.
- Managers find comfort in the status quo & Leaders serve as a catalyst for change & growth.
- Managers settle for industry standard & Leaders innovate beyond the standard demanding the best.
- Managers wield power while Leaders apply influence.

- Managers control & Leaders inspire.
- Managers formulate policy & Leaders set examples.
- Managers instruct...Leaders mentor.
- Managers are reactive while Leaders are proactive.
- Managers plan...Leaders innovate.
- Managers refine...Leaders revolutionize.
- Managers reorganize...Leaders reinvent.
- Managers pursue the tangible while Leaders seek the intangible.

We have all witnessed companies that have been over managed in the absence of leadership. When leadership has been abdicated to management in a corporate setting you will always find that growth slows, morale declines, creativity wanes and the competitive edge is weakened. That being said, I have personally experienced the value of true leadership at every stage of my life from the athletic playing field, to the military to the corporate boardroom. Let's look at an example of the value of leadership from each of the three areas:

• An example from the world of athletics...If you were the owner of an NFL franchise and had to choose between having the #1 quarterback in the league or the #1 center in league what would your choice be? Again this doesn't mean that a great center isn't valuable, it just means that the role player isn't as valuable to the team as having the talent factor and leadership characteristics of a true impact player. Simply reflect back upon your own life experiences and you'll see that you have come across many utility players over the years, but very few franchise players.

• A military example...Contrast if you will the

differences of two enlisted men of the same rank. The first is a sergeant in a headquarters unit charged with the administrative support of a company commander. The second sergeant is a combat controller in a special operations unit charged with coordinating air strikes from the ground behind enemy lines. While both of the enlisted men described above hold the same rank, are part of a team, and play important roles, one is clearly an impact player in a leadership capacity while the other is solely a utility player acting in a management capacity. The military has determined that it is a rare individual who exhibits the characteristics necessary to become a member of a special operations unit. Therefore they are willing to make a much larger investment in the combat controller and in return the military expects a much larger contribution from that individual.

• A corporate example...This example will be short and sweet, but hopefully very clear in its statement of impact. Who do you believe is of greater value and makes a larger contribution to a corporation, someone who administers policy and creates processes or someone who sets the vision and creates the strategy? Just examine the difference in the pay stubs of the two individuals contrasted above and you'll quickly see who the enterprise deems to be of higher value.

I want to be clear that I am not "anti" manager. I am however very "pro" leadership when it comes to optimizing the talent factor in any organization. My bias toward leadership doesn't mean that I don't understand the principles behind such truisms as: "there is no "I" in team" or, that "a chain is only as strong as its weakest link." Rather it simply means that I believe you achieve a much greater return on human capital with investments made into leadership due to the scope and scale of the impact that a leader can make. The bottom line is that I prefer to lead rather than manage and to be led rather than to be managed.

Now that we've defined the difference between leaders and managers lets do a deeper dive on what it takes to be an effective leader. In thinking about all the conversations and debates over the years on the topic of leadership I noticed an interesting paradox...while there are vehement disagreements on the effectiveness (or lack thereof) of different leadership styles, most people are in agreement on the qualities and attributes possessed by great leaders regardless of style. In further pondering this dichotomy an interesting thought came to mind...If I could genetically engineer the perfect leadership gene what qualities and characteristics would constitute the architecture of leadership DNA?

In attempting to paint the portrait of the perfect leader I asked myself what traits would my perfect leader possess? Courage, vision, wisdom, integrity, empathy, persistence, compassion, aggressivity, discernment, commitment, confidence, a bias to action, creativity, self-discipline, loyalty, confidence, a great strategic thinker, passion, intelligence, humility, great communication skills, common sense, generosity, the ability to identify and develop great talent, attention to detail, faith, an active listener, respect for others, an excellent tactician, charisma, extreme focus, a high tolerance for risk, a broad range of competencies, and the list goes on...

By the way, if any of you possess all the above attributes please forward your resume to my attention! All kidding aside, the longer my list of desirable qualities became, the more I realized the frivolity of this exercise...There is no perfect leader only the right leader for a given situation. As I've addressed in other parts of the book, great leaders have the innate ability to call on the right skills in a contextually and environmentally appropriate fashion. No single leader can possess every needed attribute. If I were successful in my genetic engineering exercise I would no doubt have created a leader who would be driven crazy by emotional and intellectual conflicts.

Now that I've explained why it's impossible to possess every one of the leadership traits known to mankind, let's turn our attention to a few other observations and conclusions that I've drawn over the years. These thoughts are some of the less talked about, yet some of the most important traits that you must possess in order to become a great leader and an outstanding CEO.

FOLLOW THROUGH

"When you get right down to root of the meaning of the word *succeed*, you find that is simply means to follow through."
- F.W. Nichol

While this seems like a pretty basic concept you'd be surprised at how many leaders fail based upon this issue alone. When I was just starting out in business one of my original mentors told me "to just do what you say you're going to do, and that in and of itself will place you in a very select group within the business world." When I was younger it seemed impossible to me that doing something so basic could lead to great success. Well, now that I'm older and more experienced all I can say is "how right he was!" It never ceases to amaze me at the number of people that fail to deliver on their commitments. The old cliché of "over-promising and under-delivering" has sadly become all too commonplace in the business world. Is it really that hard to fulfill on promises made? So my question to you is this…Can you, and do you walk the talk?

So inexorably interwoven into the fabric of today's business culture is this trend that I frequently observe people who have actually come to expect failure. Furthermore, when said failure occurs, it is accepted as usual and customary practice. It is the failure to follow through that blows-up transactions, causes employees to seek work elsewhere, sends what were once loyal customers running to the competition and it can send even the strongest of brands into decline.

Failure is not necessarily a bad thing in and of itself. In fact, I have always learned more from my failures than I have my successes. However, accepting failure, not learning from failure, or failing through apathy or ignorance, are all corporate killers. As a person in a position of authority make sure that you set the chinning bar very high. Expect great things of people, equip them to succeed and don't ever accept failure as being okay. When the inevitable failures do occur conduct a failure analysis to determine what went wrong and why, transfer the knowledge gained across the enterprise and move on to more fertile ground.

Some people don't follow through simply because they are lazy and it is just easier to deal with the consequences of not following through than it is to actually invest the effort in getting the job done. Have you ever experienced the individuals who just tell you what they think you want to hear? These people fall into two distinct categories. The first category is the people pleaser. These individuals don't like conflict and will say or do just about anything to avoid it. They believe if they tell you what you want to hear long enough that it will either come true or that you'll just go away and either one is okay by them. The second category is comprised of the darker side of business. These are the individuals that will say or do anything to initially get your business, but once they have separated you from your money they could care less about what was said before the sale. In either case (well intentioned or otherwise) beware of those individuals that appear to be just saying what you want to hear as trouble will surely follow.

Sadly, all it really takes to stand out in corporate America is to follow the direction of my mentor and just do what you say you'll do...It doesn't matter where you went to school, how smart you are, what your title is or any number of other considerations, if you want to succeed learn to honor your commitments and execute. Perhaps the most important aspect of good follow through is that it creates credibility and a bond of trust. People trust those individuals that fulfill their obligations and don't tend to trust those who fail to deliver. I am a perfect example of someone who has probably achieved more success in business than deserved by simply doing nothing more than honoring my commitments...I say what I mean...I mean what I say...I do what I say I'm going to do. It is just not that hard to follow through.

DOING THE RIGHT THING

"Integrity is doing the right thing, even if nobody is watching"

- Unknown

One of my favorite business theorists was the late Peter Drucker. Dr. Drucker passed away back in 2005, but prior to his death he authored more than 35 books and is considered by many to be the founding father on the study of management practices. In the text that follows I will breakdown one of my favorite "Druckerisms" which states that: "managers do things right while leaders do the right things."

At first glance the above Druckerism might not seem to be all that insightful, but I believe it is a very powerful observation that highlights the difference in philosophies between most managers and leaders.

Doing things right is a trait that causes many managers to be focused on security which is often underpinned by fear based motivations. Doing things right will drive managers toward a position of being safe and politically correct in their approach to business. It is this fear based motivation that causes managers to protect turf as opposed to gain ground, to control as opposed to inspire, and to refine as opposed to create. Doing things right leads to comfort zone management that completely inhibits the ability to innovate.

Doing the right things is a trait that causes leaders to be guided by their instincts, principles, values and desire to achieve. Leaders motivated by doing the right things are not risk adverse, rarely politically correct and they thrive on shaking things up. It is leaders doing the right things that innovate, motivate, create and inspire. Doing the right thing is often times controversial, but true leaders are not daunted by the thought of conflict as are most managers. Leaders guided by doing the right thing are willing to step-up and make the big decisions that open markets, exploit opportunities, and drive innovation. If you're not sure whether you are doing things right or doing the right things take yourself through the following personal assessment:

1. When was the last time you witnessed something that you didn't agree with but kept quiet on the issue to protect yourself or your position rather than voicing your concern in order to protect the enterprise?
2. When was the last time you rocked the boat by design? Rocking the boat by default or by mistake doesn't count...
3. When was the last time you drove innovation? Hint: purchasing a new software application is not innovation...
4. If a survey was taken of your peers and subordinates would they refer to you as a leader who inspires, motivates and mentors or a manager who exercises authority and control?

It is important to realize that everyone has fears. Ask anyone who has ever been in combat and they'll tell you that it is being in touch with their innate sense of fear that kept them alive. However as important as it is to be aware of your fears, as a leader you cannot allow yourself to be ruled by them. Don't "just do it", rather just "do the right thing" and watch your successes multiply.

CONTEXTUAL THINKING

"The ability to lead and think contextually is what creates success across constituencies regardless of emotions or positions"

- Mike Myatt

The ability to think contextually is a necessary skill set

for all CEOs seeking to operate at the top of their game. It has been said that the only constant in life is change. Given that change is bound to occur it is surprising the small number of CEOs that actually excel at leading change. Static thinking in a vacuum that does not take into account situational and contextual nuances will leave even the most experienced leaders wondering what went wrong...

I have met brilliant linear thinkers who given the right environment, or enough time, could come up with the correct solution to most problems. However, in today's world, environments are ever changing and cycle times are ever compressing. The need to quickly make situational assessments has never been more critical for leaders as decisions that could once be made over a matter of weeks and months now often times need to be made in a matter of hours.

The mantra of "Adapt, Improvise and Overcome" was drilled into me during my years in the military. Failure was not an option and the ability to deal with mission critical decisioning on short time frames was a mandatory skill for survival. The same is true in business today. Great leaders must be able to take B-school academic theory and traditional business logic and adapt them to the context of the situation at hand. Contextual thinking is a more refined version of "thinking outside the box." Being capable of getting outside the business of business and dealing with issues of relationships, culture, politics, innovation, creativity, accountability and tactical precision are the skills needed to catalyze growth and create a sustainable enterprise.

One size fits all leadership styles restrict the effectiveness of professionals, alienate staff and peers and limit the ability of a company to thrive in ever changing markets. Companies led by traditional executives whose leadership style hasn't kept pace with current practices will be left behind by competition that understands the need to apply situational velocity within a contextual framework. The bottom line is that your ability as a leader to authentically adapt your style situationally and contextually will have a direct correlation to the level of success you achieve in today's business world.

So important is the topic of context that I want to offer you a case study on the topic to demonstrate what can happen when you lose sight of context. The case study I've chosen will be one of certain controversy as it picks on what I believe to be flawed logic contained in one of the most popular business books of the last decade: "Good To Great" by Jim Collins.

Let me begin by saying that I am generally speaking a fan of Jim Collins and his work, and that I enjoyed reading "Good To Great". I believe there is a plethora of quality information to be gleaned from the pages of "Good To Great," but I also believe there are some potentially dangerous and misleading concepts/principles that can cause great harm to a business if taken out of **context**.

Jim Collins and his research staff are truly dedicated and talented professionals who have completed volumes of quality research on what it takes to build an enduring and successful enterprise. That being said, the key to understanding, validating and appropriately applying any form of research is to understand the **context** in which it was developed as well as the business logic that was used to frame it.

The problem with "Good To Great" is that the reader is left with the false impression that the principles contained in the book can be universally transferred to their individual situation without regard for **context**. The reader

41

is led to believe that if they apply the principles contained in the book to their business that the results will mirror those of the companies examined in the book, and that their business will in turn make the leap from good to great and enjoy sustaining good fortune. This is simply not true…You see all research, even good research (as Jim's is), must be evaluated **contextually**. There are very few universal truths in business that can be applied in a vacuum.

In the text below I will examine what I believe to be three of the most critical flaws in business logic contained in "Good To Great":

1. The Study Itself: The study in and of itself has a bias in that it evaluated 22 Fortune 500 Companies. The study compared and contrasted 11 companies that made the transition from good to great and 11 peer companies that did not. The problem with this study is that it applies to a very small universe. How many of you reading this book are currently CEO's of Fortune 500 companies? Fortune 500 companies are mature, well branded, well capitalized, already successful companies. To assume that a start-up, small, mid-size or even relatively large company can adopt the business practices of Fortune 500 companies is just not realistic. Adopting this line of thinking in a vacuum can actually send a company into a death spiral due to a lack of **contextual** benchmarking.

2. Level Five Leaders: Jim refers to a hierarchical matrix of leadership that describes 5 different types of leaders and suggests that only with rare exception can anything other than a level 5 leader take a company from good to great. While I agree with many of his suppositions on what makes a great leader, I vehemently disagree that only one leadership style can work effectively. I have personally witnessed just about every style of leader both succeed and fail. While I find some leadership styles more pleasant than others to adopt, developing a "one size fits all" mentality toward what it takes to lead a company is a huge mistake. It is not the leadership style in a vacuum that is as important as selecting the right leader based upon aligning style with the environmental, situational and **contextual** circumstances of the time along with the mission at hand.

3. The Flywheel and the Doom Loop: Jim's theory here is that "those who launch radical change programs and wrenching restructurings will almost certainly fail to make the leap" (from good to great). While I am a strong believer in the flywheel principal as a general practice there are also times when radical change is in fact the critical element needed to move a company to the next level of success. It is not change or reengineering that are the evils, rather it is ill-conceived or poorly implemented change that can cause harm. Beware the change agents for the sake of change, but embrace change by design (radical or otherwise) for the good of the enterprise. When a business strategy is applied based upon **contextually** appropriate business logic it will succeed, and taken out of **context** it will fail.

There are two primary differences between Jim's view of the world and mine: 1) Jim's conclusions are drawn largely from historical research conducted in the classroom and think-tank and my conclusions are drawn from hands-on, in the trenches experience, and; 2) Jim believes that his data is applicable to virtually any situation in business and I believe everything must be evaluated against the situational, environmental and **contextual** aspects of any given scenario. Assuming that all formulas are made up of constants without consideration for the inevitable set of variables that always come into play is just not sound thinking.

GREAT LEADERS MAKE GREAT DECISIONS

"In any moment of decision the best thing you can do is the right thing, the next best thing is the wrong thing, and the worst thing you can do is nothing."
- Theodore Roosevelt

Great leaders who rise to the C-suite do so largely based upon their ability to consistently make sound decisions. However while it may take years of solid decision making to reach the boardroom it often times only takes one bad decision to fall from the ivory tower. The reality is that in today's competitive business world an executive is only as good as his/her last decision. The text that follows is designed to provide you with a framework for making consistently good decisions...

Nothing will test your metal as a CEO more than your ability to make decisions. I happen to be the type of person that would rather make the decision than have to live with someone else's decisions. In fact I absolutely love to make decisions and whether it is in my role in the business world, or my role as a husband and father, I want to be the one making the tough calls. That being said, nobody is immune to bad decisioning...We have all made bad decisions whether we like to admit it or not. Show me someone who hasn't made a bad decision and I'll show you someone who is either not being honest or someone who avoids decisioning at all costs.

For more than 20 years I have either served in the capacity of a professional advisor, principal owner or senior executive and have generally been highly regarded for my decision making ability. Like everyone else I have also made some regrettable decisions along the way. When I reflect back upon the poor decisions I've made it's not that I wasn't

44

capable of making the correct decision, but for whatever reason I failed to use sound decisioning methodology. Gut instincts can only take you so far in life and anyone who operates outside of a sound decisioning framework will eventually fall prey to an act of oversight, misinformation, misunderstanding, manipulation, impulsivity or some other negative influencing factor.

The complexity of the current business landscape combined with ever increasing expectations of performance and the speed at which decisions must be made are a potential recipe for disaster for today's CEO unless a defined methodology for decisioning is put into place. If you incorporate the following metrics into your decisioning framework you will minimize the chances of making a bad decision:

1. **Perform a Situation Analysis**: What is motivating the need for a decision? Who will the decision impact (both directly and indirectly)? What data, analytics, research or supporting information do you have to validate your decision?

2. **Subject your Decision to Public Scrutiny**: There are no private decisions...Sooner or later the details surrounding any decision will likely come out. If your decision were printed on the front page of the newspaper how would you feel? What would your family think of your decision? How would your shareholders and employees feel about your decision? Have you sought counsel and/or feedback before making your decision?

3. **Conduct a Cost/Benefit Analysis**: Do the potential benefits derived from the decision justify the expected costs? What if the costs exceed projections and the benefits fall short of projections?

4. **Assess the Risk/Reward Ratio**: What are all the

possible rewards and when contrasted with all the potential risks are the odds in your favor or are they stacked against you?

5. **Assess Whether it is the Right Thing To Do**: Standing behind decisions that everyone supports doesn't particularly require a lot of chutzpa. On the other hand, standing behind what one believes is the right decision in the face of tremendous controversy is the stuff great leaders are made of. My wife has always told me that "you can't go wrong by going right" and as usual I find her advice to be spot on...Never compromise your value system, your character or your integrity.

6. **Make The Decision**: Perhaps most importantly you must have a bias toward action and be willing to make the decision. Moreover as a CEO you must learn to make the best decision possible even if you possess an incomplete data set. Don't fall prey to analysis paralysis but rather make the best decision possible with the information at hand using some of the methods mentioned above. Opportunities are not static and the law of diminishing returns applies to most opportunities in that the longer you wait to seize the opportunity the smaller the return typically is. In fact, more likely is the case that the opportunity will completely evaporate if you wait too long to seize it.

Part of learning to make great decisions is developing critical thinking skills that can be leveraged as part of your decisioning metrics. Great CEOs possess outstanding critical thinking skills. The following items represent the 10 most common critical thinking errors:

1. **Absolutes**: Avoid thinking in extremes, overgeneralizations, or stereotypes. When you think in terms of "always" and "never" you are not thinking clearly. There are few absolutes in life and thinking in these terms

will limit your options and set you up for failure.

2. **Awfulizing**: Thinking from a pessimistic point of view will cripple your ability to make sound decisions. Don't be guilty of making a mountain out of a mole-hill or viewing things from a glass is half empty perspective. Few people will tolerate a person that habitually awfulizes their situation.

3. **Blaming**: If you have the tendency to transfer responsibility to others for your thoughts, emotions and behaviors you are guilty of being a blamer. Stop pointing fingers at others and accept responsibility for your own thoughts and actions.

4. **I Can't**: Very few things in life are a result of situations where you "can't" accomplish something. Rather the term "can't" is a subconscious translation for "I don't want to" or "I'm not willing to put forth the effort to." Extricate the word can't from your thoughts and your vocabulary.

5. **Desires**: Similar to "I Can't" the desire for something is rarely synonymous with the need for something. Thinking in terms of what you desire is usually nothing more than a cop-out. What you "want" vs. what you "need" are rarely one in the same. There is nothing wrong with wanting or desiring something so long as these thoughts are not confused with needs.

6. **Try**: This is another word to remove from your thought process and your vocabulary. Using the word try is simply demonstrating an avoidance of commitment that is a set-up for failure.

7. **Misunderstanding of Fact**: Confusing fact with fiction is a dangerous habit. Just because you want something to be true doesn't mean that it is. Avoid stating opinion as fact, and don't disregard the opinions of others simply because they differ from yours.

8. **Should**: Yet another word or thought to be avoided. The world certainly owes you nothing and the truth is that very few people owe you anything either. Placing unrealistic demands on yourself or others as well as having unrealistic thoughts will tend to polarize as opposed to align.

9. **Minimizing Negative Outcomes**: While it's very common for CEOs to have a high tolerance for risk, that's not the same thing as purposefully choosing to disregard possible consequences. Right thinking requires that risks must be identified, assessed and managed in order to avoid unnecessary disasters.

10. **Thinking in a Vacuum**: Thinking in isolation, not assessing options and alternatives, and not seeking counsel has resulted in many a poor decision. Great leaders accept almost nothing at face value rather they challenge and question everything.

Decisions can, and usually will, make or break a CEO. Those that avoid making decisions solely for fear of making a bad decision will rarely rise above mid-management, and those that make decisions just for the sake of making a decision will likely not last too long in the world of business. If you develop the appropriate blend of a bias to action with an analytical approach to decisioning your stock as a CEO will surely rise.

GREAT LEADERS UNDERSTAND THE USE OF INFLUENCE

"The greatest ability in business is to get along with others and to influence their actions"
- John Hancock

As a CEO your "Influence Quotient" is the IQ you need

to pay attention to. Your influence quotient will be a much greater determinant of your ultimate success than your "Intelligence Quotient" could ever be. Innate, raw intelligence while certainly something to be prized is much more common and much less powerful than real influence.

When I speak about influence I'm not talking about manipulation, elaborate schemes or other forms of skullduggery. Ill-gotten gains will always be exposed for what they are, and will never be worth the compromises that were made in order to achieve them. Not only is true influence much easier to acquire, but it is also sustainable. Put simply, true influence is nothing more than understanding how to work with and through others to achieve a stated objective while staying true to your core values and maintaining your integrity.

I make my living largely based upon influence. In my world influence equals leverage... It is my ability to be able to work effectively with, and through, many people spanning industries, specialties, and geographies that allow me to get things done on behalf of my clients. Absent understanding how to create powerful spheres of influence, my world would be limited to what I could accomplish on my own, which would be only a small fraction of what my network is able to accomplish.

The following fundamental concepts of influence which if properly understood and implemented can help anyone become more efficient, productive, secure and successful:

1. Influence is built upon making others successful: This is often times referred to as the law of reciprocity. The theory is that if you invest yourself in making someone else successful then they in turn will likely be predisposed to helping you become successful. While this principle will not always pan out, in my experience it has held true in well over 90% of my interactions over the years.

2. Likeability: People do business with people they like and avoid doing business with people they don't like…it's just that simple. Are you approachable, positive, affable, trustworthy, a person of character and integrity or are you someone who is standoffish, pessimistic and generally not to be trusted? Those that fall into the camp of the former as opposed to the latter will find themselves having more influence and success.

3. Influence is wielded through helping others maintain commitments: Professionals respect other professionals who keep their commitments. In the business world you are most often judged on your ability to keep your word and deliver on your promises. The key behind influencing people via commitment lies in your ability to have people adopt an initial position that is consistent with a behavior such that they are willing to agree to requests that are consistent with their prior commitment. People desire to be perceived as dependable, reliable and successful and will normally go to great lengths not to have their track-record or reputation tarnished. Gain strong commitments early on and simply hold people to their commitments. This ultimately helps them enhance their reputation for delivering on promises made.

4. Influence is most often possessed by those with authority: It is important to realize that the highest authority is that which is given and rarely that which is taken. Authority is most often given to those that display honesty, competency, expertise and wisdom. With authority comes credibility and with credibility comes influence. While influence can be wielded by those without authority it will be limited in both scope and scale. Those with the most authority will always have the most influence.

5. Value and scarcity drive influence: Understanding

the value of your position, brand, authority, resources, access to people or knowledge and any number of other items as it relates to fulfilling the needs and desires of others creates influence. To the extent that anything under your direct or indirect control is scarce or proprietary your ability to influence will increase significantly.

Bottom line...Don't manipulate for personal gain rather facilitate for mutual benefit. Take a sincere interest in the success of others, work on your likeability factor, become adept at gaining commitment, develop your authority and control and have access to things of value or scarcity and your influence with others will increase.

UNDERSTANDING YOUR STRENGTHS AND WEAKNESSES

"If you think weakness can be turned into a strength, I hate to tell you this, but that's another weakness"
- Jack Handy

Should you play to your strengths or shore-up your weaknesses? If you pose this question to a group of professionals, some will answer play to your strengths, some will answer shore-up your weaknesses, and others will answer both. The truth is that they are all correct to a degree...The real answer lies in understanding context, environment and priority. Continued professional growth leading to increased performance over time is what separates the average leaders from the great leaders. Rapidly evolving markets demand that successful business people have fluidity in their approach to professional development. However many CEOs focus on the wrong areas, at the wrong times and for the wrong reasons in their efforts to refine and improve their skill sets.

Focus needs to be applied to areas that can have the greatest impact on your performance as a leader. It is nothing short of foolishness to waste time, energy or capital on improving weaknesses that don't matter. Unless a weakness creates a barrier between you and the completion of your mission, or impedes you from utilizing your strengths it is not really a weakness that needs to be addressed.

As an example, if you are a CEO with poor interpersonal communication skills which prohibit you from being able to articulately and persuasively sell the corporate vision you should immediately go to work on improving your communication ability. By way of contrast, if you're a CEO who has poor administrative skills, who cares? It is likely that as CEO you have unfettered access to administrative support to which you can delegate activities that are not highest and best use to begin with, so why worry about how to send a fax, filing nomenclature, how to fix a jammed photocopier or how to work the scanner?

It is critical that you understand it takes much more dedication, determination and energy to go from poor to mediocre than it does to move from good to excellent. It is also important to check your motivation and interest level in determining which areas you desire to improve upon. If you're not passionate about something it is difficult to be motivated and without motivation it is virtually impossible to maintain any interest. As a busy executive you only have so much time in a day so don't waste it on areas that do not add value or create leverage.

Those of you who are familiar with my philosophy understand the importance of focus. However as important as focus is, of equal or greater importance is what you choose to focus on. As mentioned above focus needs to be brought to bear on issues that stand between where you are and where you want to go. Understanding how to identify barriers is mission critical to your ability to succeed in business. Barriers are best identified as things that can be removed though acquiring influence (being able to leverage the right sphere of influence when needed), knowledge (training, continuing education, self-learning, etc.), improving skills (training, practice, focus) and gaining experience (broadening roles, more tenure, being mentored, etc.).

Bottom line...Focused professional development requires: 1) Motivation to improve; 2) the ability to identify barriers; 3) determining the proper method of removing the barrier by improving skill sets, acquiring knowledge or gaining experience, and; 4) Conducting a cost/benefit and risk/reward assessment to determine whether the barrier needs to be addressed immediately, over the mid-range or the long-term.

BECOME A GREAT COMMUNICATOR

"Great communicators have an appreciation for positioning. They understand the people they're trying to reach and what they can and can't hear."
- John Kotter

The key to becoming a skillful communicator is rarely found in what you have been classically taught in the academic world. Rather the truth is hidden in what they don't teach you about communications that you desperately need to know in order to thrive as a leader and to become an effective CEO... From our earliest days in the classroom we are trained to focus on annunciation, vocabulary, presence, delivery, grammar, syntax and the like, but it is the more subtle elements of communication that separate the truly great communicators from those that bumble and stumble through their interactions with others.

Most professionals will typically spend more than 80% of their time each day in some type of an interpersonal situation; thus it is no surprise to find that a large number of organizational problems occur as a result of poor communications. Effective communication is an essential component of becoming a successful leader whether it is at the interpersonal, intergroup, intragroup, organizational, or external levels. Developing an understanding of great communication skills is easier than one might think; however being able to appropriately draw upon said skills when the chips are down is not always as easy as one might hope for. Skills acquired and/or knowledge gained is only valuable to the extent that they can be practically applied when called for.

It has been my experience that the number one thing that great communicators have in common is that they possess a heightened sense of situational and contextual awareness (are you noticing a consistent theme?). The best communicators are great listeners and even better observers. Great communicators can read a person/group by sensing the moods, dynamics, attitudes, values and concerns of those being spoken to. Not only do they read the environment well, but they possess the uncanny ability to adapt their messaging to said environment without missing a beat. The message is not about the speaker...It has nothing to do with the speaker...It is however 100% about meeting the needs and the expectations of those you're speaking to.

So let's start by breaking down the construct of a good message. You've all heard the saying "it's not what you say, but how you say it that matters" and while there is surely an element of truth in that statement I'm here to tell you that it matters very much what you say. Good communicators address both the "what" and "how" aspects of messaging so that they don't fall prey to becoming the smooth talker who leaves people with the impression of form over substance...The key is to base the foundation of your message in the following three areas:

1. Possess Accurate and Authoritative Information: Develop a technical command over your subject matter. If you don't possess subject matter expertise few people will give you the time of day...Most successful people have little interest in listening to those individuals that cannot add value to a situation or topic but force themselves into a conversation just to hear themselves speak. The fake it until you make it days have long sense passed and for most people I know fast and slick equals not credible...

2. Specificity is better than Ambiguity 11 times out of 10: Learn to deliver your message with clarity. Simple and concise is better than complicated and confusing. Time has never been a more precious commodity that it is in today's marketplace. It is critical that you know how to cut to the chase and hit the high points. Without understanding the value of brevity and clarity it is unlikely that you'll ever be afforded the opportunity to get to the granular level as you'll lose the floor long before you ever get there...

3. Be Able to Communicate the Same Message in a Number of Different Ways: If your expertise and clarity don't have the effect you hope for you need to be able to make an impact by adding style elements to your message to make sure that it is understood and is well received. Use humor, stories, analogies, case studies and bold statements to paint powerful word pictures that educate, inform, entice and motivate. While it is sometimes necessary to "Shock and Awe" this tactic should be reserved as a last resort. Great leaders are almost always great story tellers. They frequently communicate in vignettes that help people connect the dots while being entertained and staying engaged in the message.

Another component of communications strategy that is rarely discussed is how to prevent a message from going bad and what to do when does. It's called being prepared and developing a contingency plan...While you clearly need to begin by keeping your focus on the objective (communicate, persuade, gather information, motivate, educate, solicit, etc.) you must keep in mind that for your agenda to gain traction your objective must be in alignment with those you are communicating with.

Don't assume that someone is ready to have a particular conversation with you just because you're ready to have the conversation with them. Spending time paving the way for a productive conversation is far better than coming off as the proverbial bull in a china shop. Furthermore you cannot assume that someone knows where you're coming from if you don't tell them. I never ceased to be amazed at how many people assume that everyone knows what they want to occur without ever finding it necessary to communicate the objective...If you fail to justify your message with knowledge, business logic, reason etc. you will find that said message will likely fall on deaf ears needing reinforcement or clarification afterwards.

CEOs who are great communicators use both their verbal and non-verbal communication skills to effectively manage tough relationships and to excel at conflict resolution. Anyone who has ever been in a leadership position has had to deal with the inevitable tough relationship that causes more than its fair share of brain damage. At some point in time we've all been involved (directly or indirectly, willingly and unwillingly) in the corporate politics of turf-wars, empire building, silo-centric ignorance, title inflated ego, arrogance etc. Regardless of the politics in play, it is a CEOs responsibility to effectively lead not only those that agree with their position, but they must also lead those that hold dissenting opinions.

There are always those who choose to oppose or undermine authority but it does not remove the obligation of a chief executive to fulfill his or her duty. While likeability is a great asset to possess as a CEO, it is not essential. It is however essential that you earn the respect of those you lead. Respect is earned by honoring commitments and doing the right thing regardless of opinion, sentiment or influence. It is through right acts, good decisions and honest communication that you earn respect and maintain rapport even with those who are not necessarily your greatest supporters.

A key point to consider when things don't seem to be going as smoothly as you would like is that different perspectives, competing agendas and opposing positions can sometimes present the opportunity for growth and enlightenment. If differing opinions are looked at as an opportunity as opposed to a set-back then I believe positive steps can be taken. What I like to refer as "positional gaps" are best closed by listening to both sides, finding common ground and then letting the principle of doing the right thing guide the process. When you develop the skill to transform negative conflict into creative tension then you will begin to gain respect even from those who don't agree with your positions.

It is absolutely possible to build very productive relationships with even the most adversarial of individuals. Regardless of a person's original intent, opinion or position, the key to closing a positional gap is simply a matter of finding common ground in order to establish rapport. Moreover, building rapport is easily achieved assuming your motivations for doing so are sincere. I have always found that rapport is quickly developed when you listen, care and attempt to help people succeed. By way of contrast it is difficult to build rapport if you are driven by an agenda that is not in alignment with the other party...

While building and maintaining rapport with people with whom you disagree is certainly more challenging, many of the same rules expressed in my comments above still apply. I have found that often times conflict resolution simply just requires more intense focus on understanding the needs, wants and desires of the other party. If opposing views are worth the time and energy to debate then they are worth a legitimate effort to gain alignment on perspective and resolution on position. However this will rarely happen if lines of communication do not remain open, and candid, effective communication is best maintained through a mutual respect and rapport.

In an attempt to resolve any conflict the first step is to identify and isolate the specific areas of difference being debated. The sad fact is that many business people are absolutists in that they only see things in terms of rights and wrongs. Thinking in terms of "my way" is right and therefore "other ways" are wrong is the basis for polarizing any relationship which quickly results in converting discussions into power struggles. However when a situation can be seen through the lens of difference, and a position is simply a matter of opinion not a totalitarian statement of fact, then cooperation and compromise is possible. Identifying and understanding differences allows people (regardless of title) to shift their position through compromise and negotiation while maintaining respect and rapport. The following perspectives if kept top of mind will help in identifying and bridging positional gaps:

- Respect leads to acceptance.
- Accepting a person where they are, creates an bond of trust.
- Trust, leads to a willingness to be open to:
  - new opportunities;
  - new collaborations;
  - new strategies;
  - new ideas, and;
  - new solutions.

While I like to think that I have earned the respect of the majority of those I have led over the years, I am not so naive to think that that all have liked or supported my positions...that being said, I have nonetheless had to lead them as well. You see it is the very bane of human existence, which is in fact human nature itself that will always create gaps in thinking and philosophy and no matter how much we all wish it wasn't so...it is. So the question then becomes how to effectively deal with conflict when it arises.

It is essential for organizational health and performance that conflict be accepted and addressed through effective conflict resolution processes. While having a conflict resolution structure is important, effective utilization of conflict resolution processes is ultimately dependant upon the ability of all parties to understand the benefits of conflict resolution and perhaps more importantly their desire to resolve the matter. The following tips will help to more effectively handle conflicts in the workplace:

1. Seek out and identify conflict before it escalates...hit it head on. While you can't always prevent conflicts it has been my experience that the secret to conflict resolution is in fact conflict prevention where possible. By actually seeking out areas of potential conflict

and proactively intervening in a fair and decisive fashion you will likely prevent certain conflicts from ever arising, and if a conflict does flair up, you will likely minimize its severity by dealing with it quickly.

2. Say what you mean, mean what you say and follow-through on your commitments;

3. Never be swayed by consensus rather be guided by doing the right thing;

4. Know that no person is universally right or universally liked and become at peace with that;

5. Regardless of whether or not perspectives and opinions differ, a position of respect must be adhered to and maintained. Respect is at the core of building business relationships. It is the foundation that supports high performance teams, partnerships, as well as superior, subordinate and peer-to-peer relationships. Respecting the right to differ while being productive is a concept that all successful CEOs learn to master;

6. You know what they say about assuming…Define acceptable behavior. Just having a definition for what constitutes acceptable behavior is a positive step in avoiding conflict. Creating a framework for decisioning, using a published delegation of authority statement, encouraging best practices in collaboration, team building, leadership development and talent management will all help avoid conflicts. Having clearly defined job descriptions so that people know what's expected of them and a well articulated chain of command to allow for effective communication will also help avoid conflicts;

7. Understanding the other professionals WIIFM (What's In It For Me) position is critical. It is absolutely essential to understand other's motivations prior to weighing in. The way to avoid conflict is to help those around you achieve their objectives. If you approach

conflict from the perspective of taking the action that will help others best achieve their goals you will find few obstacles will stand in your way with regard to resolving conflict, and;

8. Pick your battles and avoid conflict for the sake of conflict. However if the issue is important enough to create a conflict then it is surely important enough to resolve. If the issue, circumstance or situation is important enough and there is enough at stake people will do what is necessary to open lines of communication and close positional gaps.

Bottom line...I believe resolution can normally be found with conflicts where there is a sincere desire to do so. Turning the other cheek, compromise, forgiveness, compassion, empathy, finding common ground, being an active listener, service above self and numerous other approaches will always allow one to be successful in building rapport if the underlying desire is strong enough. The leadership lesson here is that whenever you have a message to communicate (either directly or indirectly through a third party) make sure that said message is well reasoned such that it can be substantiated by solid business logic that is specific, consistent, clear and accurate. Spending a little extra time on the front-end of the messaging curve will likely save you from considerable aggravation and brain damage on the back-end.

DEVELOPING A PRESENCE

"It is implied in all superior cultures that a complete man would need no auxiliaries to his personal presence"
- Ralph Waldo Emerson

Can you be a true leader without possessing a command

presence? In my experience, very rarely... I'm not referencing the wannabe leaders oozing bravado, false confidence, arrogance or self-delusion spun as confidence. Nor am I referring to the weak, innocuous or timid that while viewing themselves as leaders are perhaps the farthest thing from a leader. Rather I'm addressing those true leaders who inspire and motivate those around them to achieve things well beyond that which they thought themselves capable of.

Command presence is a military term which describes someone who is instantaneously recognized as a person of authority...someone who is to be respected and followed. How much will your peers and subordinates sacrifice to follow you? Command presence has nothing to do with leadership style or approach, but it has everything to do with how you are perceived by those around you.

When you walk into a room does anyone notice? When you speak does anyone listen? When you give direction is it respected and followed? Do you inspire confidence and engender credibility with those whom you come into contact with? Are people not only willing to be led by you but proud to be led by you? Command presence is far more than just the attitude you bring to the game...it's about the combination of charisma, character, integrity, knowledge and experience that separates true leaders from the masses.

During the course of my career I've observed all kinds of leaders good and bad...However I've never been around a great leader that doesn't possess strong command presence. Great leaders display an air of calm about them regardless of the situation at hand. Great leaders show co-workers that they will always maintain control even when they don't have an immediate solution. Great leaders don't lose focus, they don't cower and they never waffle.

Today's CEOs have literally hundreds of interpersonal

interactions each and everyday. Any leader who fails to instill confidence amongst subordinates will lose their loyalty, harm their morale and cripple their ability to execute. The impact of command presence is not only limited to your co-workers, but to everyone with whom you come in contact with. Your command presence or lack thereof will also impact the success of your relationships with investors, lenders, partners, suppliers, vendors and other constituencies.

Some leaders come by command presence naturally while others have to work very hard to develop it... Focus on developing the following traits in order to enhance your command presence:

1. Develop Authoritative Body Language: Note that the word authoritative does not mean intimidating, threatening or aggressive. It does however mean in charge, in control, confident, at ease and imperturbable. It all starts when you enter the room...What you wear and how you wear it, as well as how you carry yourself make a statement. Slouching, fidgeting, standing with your hands in your pockets, darting-eyes, playing with your pen, tapping your fingers on the table, hand-wringing or any other action that serves no purpose is ill advised. While possessing command presence is not about a beauty contest, it is about looking the part.

2. Develop Excellent Verbal Skills: As odd as it may sound this begins with developing excellent listening skills. You must seek to understand before you'll be understood. When it is time to speak say what you mean and mean what you say...What you say, when you say it and how you say it will both instill confidence and serve to motivate and inspire, or it will take the wind right out of your sails. You don't have to be an overly verbose person, but you must be measured and articulate. Don't speak just to hear yourself talk and don't ramble. If your verbal communication skills are not up to par get help and correct the problem. You cannot lead if you cannot communicate.

3. Make Excellent Decisions: As we've touched on before, nothing is more difficult to overcome for a leader than a poor track record. Solid decision layered upon solid decision is the key to creating loyalty. When I was serving in the military I once had a soldier under my command tell me that if I told him to attack a tank with a butter knife he would do it, because he would just assume based upon my track record that I knew something he didn't (Luckily we never had to test that theory).

Bottom line…If you develop a strong command presence, leadership while never easy, will in fact become easier.

PUT THEORY INTO ACTION

"Chaotic action is preferable to orderly inaction"
- Will Rogers

Much has been written about leadership theory, concepts, style, dynamics, what leaders are or are not and a plethora of other leadership-centric content. However my question to you is this: What is leadership without action? Theory is fine for the classroom, but in the business world theory without action is little more than useless rhetoric. Don't tell me, show me…Don't talk the talk, but walk the walk. Action is one of the elements that truly separates the wannabe leaders from the authentic leaders.

Do you have great vision? Are you a master of strategy? Do you have boundless energy or mesmerizing charisma? While the aforementioned qualities are certainly admirable, they are only valuable if they influence or create action. Walt Disney, one of the greatest creative talents and true innovators of our time realized the value of action when he said: "The way to get started is to quit talking and begin doing." Examine the truly great CEOs and you'll find that to the one they all have a strong bias toward action. Howard Schultz the Chairman of Starbucks has such a strong bias toward action that he doesn't believe in relying solely upon research to support decisioning as he says "they pay me to make decisions not to produce research." It was Andrew Grove the former Chairman and CEO of Intel and former Time Magazine Man of the Year who said "You have to take action; you can't hesitate or hedge your bets. Anything less will condemn your efforts to failure." If you can't take action, if you can't make the tough decision and if you can't instill a bias toward action in your peers and subordinates then you don't belong in a leadership position much less holding the title of CEO.

If your company has passive, timid leadership you will face serious problems in sustaining your competitive advantage. Furthermore, if your company isn't leveraging action learning to develop leaders, fuel innovation, foster collaboration and catalyze growth, then you are missing a substantial opportunity. Stop pondering and pontificating and take action.

ARE YOU EASY TO HELP

"There is no such thing as a self-made man. We are made up of thousands of others."
- George Matthew Adams

Great leaders are easy to help. Let me ask you this

question: Do you make it easy for others to want to help you or is your demeanor such that most people won't lift a finger to assist you in a time of need? How many times during the course of your career have you witnessed executives and entrepreneurs who desperately need help but either don't recognize it, or worse yet, make it virtually impossible for someone to help them? Let's examine the importance of positioning yourself to be helped...

If your pride, ego, arrogance, ignorance, the way you were raised or any other excuse (yes I did say excuse) keeps you from asking for help it is precisely those traits that will keep you from maximizing your potential. I hate to break it to you, but you don't know everything or everybody so why even bother pretending that you couldn't use a bit of help? No single person can or should go it alone in today's business world. The more partners, sympathizers, champions, allies, supporters, enablers, influencers, advisors, mentors, friends and family you have helping you succeed the faster you will achieve your goals. Without question the most successful business people on the planet are those that have learned to blow through self-imposed barriers to openly harness the power of broader spheres of influence.

I don't know about you, but I am so tired of all the "self-made man" propaganda floating around business circles. I sincerely believe there is no such thing as a "self-made man". Virtually all of the good things that have happened to me over the years have been the result of the collaborative efforts of many. I don't see asking for help as a sign of weakness, rather I see it as a very smart thing to do and I therefore tend to seek out help wherever I can find it. I have long made it a practice to encourage others to help me succeed. My personal and professional networks are far more important to my success than my individual competencies. My clients hire me not solely on the basis of what I can personally do for them in a vacuum, but rather what the collective power of my network and resources can accomplish for them when I operate outside my bubble.

If you desire to enlist others in your success the following items constitute the basic prerequisites for getting others to help you:

1. **Don't be a jerk**: While people don't necessarily have to like you in order to help you it certainly doesn't hurt. However I can promise you that if you're perceived as a jerk people will not only go out of their way not to help you succeed, but they will do everything possible to impede your success. I have long been a believer that contrary to popular opinion nice guys (and gals) do in fact finish first.

2. **Go out of your way to help others**: Do unto others - what goes around comes around - you reap what you sow, and any number of other statements to that effect tend to ring true more often than not. If you are sincerely interested in helping others and make it a habit to go out of your way to do so, then those people will likely be inclined to reciprocate.

3. **Know what you want and focus your efforts to that end**: You must develop a clear picture of what it is that you want to accomplish and then apply laser-like focus in the pursuit of your goals.

4. **Make your goals known to those that can help you**: Communicate your vision to those in a position to help you succeed and ask for their help. Don't be bashful or embarrassed, but rather confidently recruit others to become enablers and evangelizers of your cause. You need to believe that one of your top priorities is team building and consistently seek out greater numbers of people to

champion your cause and scale your efforts.

In the final analysis it's really all a matter of perspective...you can either view yourself as part of a hierarchical world sitting at the top of the org chart puffing your chest and propping-up your ego, or you can view yourself as the hub at the center of a large and diverse network. The latter is both more profitable and enjoyable than the former. You can either choose to build your personal brand and your success at the expense of others or by helping others, which means that you need to make it easy for people to want to help you by helping them.

While there are certainly other areas, traits and characteristics that are possessed by great leaders, I have covered them in other areas of the book. That being said, I want to wrap up this chapter by asking you to read one of my favorite riddles (author unknown), which poses the question; "Who am I?"

I am your constant companion. I am your greatest helper or heaviest burden. I will push you onward or drag you down to failure. I am completely at your command. Half the things you do might just as well be turned over to me and I will be able to do them quickly and correctly. I am easily managed--you must merely be firm with me. Show me exactly how you want something done and after a few lessons I will do it automatically.

I am the servant of all great people and, alas, of all failures, as well. Those who are great, I have made great. Those who are failures, I have made failures. I am not a machine, though I work with all the precision of a machine plus the intelligence of a person. You may run me for profit or run me for ruin -- if makes no difference to me. Take me, train me, be firm with me, and I will place the world at your feet. Be easy with me and I will destroy you. Who am I? *I am habit!*

As you reflect back upon what you've read thus far as well as what you continue to read in the chapters to come, think about your current behaviors, patterns, habits and constantly gut-check your motivations and actions. Great CEOs seek to eliminate bad habits and replace them with great ones...

Chapter 4

Speed, Timing & Innovation...Leading Change as a CEO

"If GM had kept up with technology like the computer
industry has, we would all be driving $25 cars that got
1000 MPG."

- Bill Gates

One of the things great CEOs must understand is that
the world around them is evolving at a very rapid
pace. As a leader you cannot hide from change rather you
must not only embrace it, but you must drive it. In the world
of athletics there is widely accepted principle that states:
"Speed Kills." In most sporting events speed will prevail
over strength and often times speed will end-up being the
deciding factor between victory and defeat. As important as
speed is on the field of play it has been my experience that it
is even more important in the world of business.

While there is little debate that speed can create an
extreme competitive advantage, it is not well understood
that the lack of speed can send a company (or a CEO's

career) into a death spiral. Agility, fluidity, decisiveness, commitment and focus all lead to the creation of speed which results in a certainty of execution. Let's examine why all CEOs should feel "The Need For Speed" if they expect to survive.

General George S. Patton said it best: "A good plan violently executed today is far and away better than a perfect plan tomorrow." The pursuit of perfection is one of the great adversaries of speed. In fact, at the risk of being controversial I'm going to take the position that perfection does not exist. I hate to break it to you, but those of you who regard yourselves as perfectionists simply exhibit perfectionistic tendencies in an unrealistic attempt to achieve what cannot be had. The pursuit of perfectionism does not result in an increase in quality, but it will result in time delays, cost overruns, missed deadlines and unfulfilled commitments. I would suggest that rather than seeking what cannot, in most cases, ever be achieved that you seek the highest standard of quality that makes economic sense, relative to the constraints of an ever shifting marketplace.

There are those that would argue that speed is synonymous with undisciplined decisioning, but I would caution you against confusing speed with reckless abandon...I'm a big proponent of planning, assessment, analysis and strategy, but only if it is concluded in a timely fashion. "Analysis Paralysis" leads to missed opportunities and failed initiatives. Over the course of my career I have consistently used speed to my personal advantage. I respond quickly via phone, IM and e-mail, I attempt to make myself available to important constituencies and I turn around detailed work product while my competitors are still in the information gathering phase. Speed is your friend...embrace it...leverage it...win with it.

Earlier in my career I served as Director of Internet

Strategy for what was at that time the world's largest web-enablement firm. While serving in that position, I coined the term "e-velocity" which we used to describe the influence that technology was having on the pace at which business had to be conducted in order to remain competitive. It used to be acceptable to take 12 to 18 months to roll-out an initiative, but in today's world you better be able to do it in 90 days or it will be obsolete before it gets to market.

When I first started in business it was usual and customary to produce 5 and 10 year business plans and today I work off of rolling 90 day tactical business plans. The latest advances in Business Process Management (BPM) have seen a reduction in the planning and budgeting cycle from 120 and 90 days to 45 days. But, is 45 days good enough? How many days constitute a responsive cycle time? Many believe the right number is between 5 and 10 days. Why is cycle time reduction important...because shorter planning and budgeting processes facilitate greater flexibility and responsiveness in meeting market demands and customer expectations. E-mail used to be the killer app and now it has become passé...My digital communication preference (along with most of my colleagues) has transitioned away from e-mail to instant messaging (IM) with IM now constituting about 70% of my messaging activity. It's all about speed...

Where many CEOs fail with regard to change initiatives is that they simply don't understand the process of change...Positive change just doesn't happen, but rather it is implemented by design. The first thing you need to do as a CEO leading change is to understand the playing field by identifying potential allies and adversaries. It is important to address the concerns and allay the fears of key influencers within your organization. When identifying who holds the power within your organization you must look well beyond the obvious senior executives. Key influencers are often not found in the executive ranks as titles alone do not equal influence. There are powerful spheres of influence that exist within your organization that may be invisible to you if you don't seek them out. These are the employees that are well liked, trusted, politically savvy, and who also don't hesitate to vocalize their opinions, even if done in stealth mode. Many a change initiative has been thwarted by individuals and groups that were either underestimated, or worse yet, never identified as spheres of influence within the company.

CEOs also need to understand that there are certain attitudes that need to be in place which serve as necessary prerequisites for change. The foundation for all positive change is honesty. There must be an authenticity and transparency surrounding the motivation for change which is clearly communicated to all those who will be touched or influenced by the proposed change.

Great CEOs understand why people resist change and take the time to address and remove potential barriers to change. Attempting to force change based upon a personal bias or prejudice is a recipe for failure. With the open and candid approach mentioned above it will be much easier to solicit buy-in from the necessary constituencies increasing your odds for success. People resent change when it comes as a surprise, and will oppose change that is forced upon them. Following are three of the most common reasons why employees will resist change:

- **No Perceived Benefit**: It's important that you can communicate the benefits of change to anyone who will be touched by the change and not just a select few. Take the time to create position statements espousing the benefits of the change to all constituencies based upon what it means to them and not you. Employees need to know how their personal situation will be improved and not just what the result is to the bottom line.

• **Fear**: Even if someone understands the benefits they may well be intimidated by the prospects of learning something new. The nature of change is that it forces people beyond their comfort zone. This can cause a high level of anxiety for many. You must communicate well beyond the benefit by addressing the personal fears and concerns of your employees. Create a transition plan that lets your employees know about timing, training, etc.

• **Ego**: If the proposed change comes across as an affront to someone's pride or ego they will become an adversary to said change. Additionally peer pressure from other employees who are opposed to the change can take otherwise supportive employees and sway their opinion.

EXPLOITING OPPORTUNITIES

"Timing is Everything"

- Unknown

The great thing about CEOs who understand how to leverage speed is that they clearly understand the relationship between speed and timing and their corresponding impact on opportunity. I've often heard people quip that they would rather be lucky than smart. While intelligence and good fortune are certainly both valuable traits to possess, neither of these traits holds a candle to having a great sense of timing...Luck is a hit or miss proposition and we've all known many a brilliant underachiever. However it has been my observation that you will rarely come across someone who possesses a great sense of timing that is anything other than successful. Let's evaluate timing as key success metric...

As the verse from the old Kenny Rogers song goes "you have to know when to hold em and know when to fold em." The reality is that great leaders all seem to possess an innate sense of timing such that most executives have a very clear understanding of the critical role timing plays as a survival skill at the C-suite level. There are a few times during the career of every CEO where staggering opportunities will present themselves. The question is not whether these opportunities exist, but rather what will you do with them when they cross your path. I believe one of the key differences between success and mediocrity is the ability to not only recognize opportunities, but also having an understanding and willingness to exploit said opportunities. Exploiting opportunities requires that CEOs not only possess vision, but also a corresponding bias to action, a bit of courage and the willingness to be disruptive in their approach to business.

Rarely will you come across a static opportunity in the sense that it will stand idle and wait for you to act...Significant opportunities are not only scarce, but they typically operate on the principal of diminishing returns. The longer you wait to seize the opportunity the smaller the return typically is. In fact, more likely is the case that the opportunity will completely evaporate if you wait too long to seize it.

I can't even begin to count the number of times I watched people miss great opportunities due to a poor sense of timing. Not too surprisingly CEOs who possess a poor sense of timing usually don't even understand timing is an issue until it's too late and they're no longer a CEO. How many times have you witnessed someone holding-out for a higher price, better valuation, evolving markets, technology advances or any number of other circumstances that either never transpire, or by the time they do the opportunistic advantage had disappeared? I've observed the risk adverse take due diligence one step too far, the greedy negotiate too long, the impulsive jump the gun, and the plodders move too slowly. As the saying goes "timing is everything."

The proverbial window closes on every opportunity at some point in time. As you approach each day I would challenge you to consistently evaluate the landscape and seize the opportunities that come your way. Better to be the one who catches the fish than the one who tells the story of the big one who got away... In any competitive business environment CEOs must quickly be able to assess risk and make timely decisions. You cannot be successful being guided by fear and hesitation. When in doubt, remember that "Speed Kills" and that "he who hesitates is lost."

TURNING SPEED AND TIMING INTO A DISRUPTIVE FOCUS

"The arrogance of success is to think that what you did yesterday will be sufficient for tomorrow"
- William Pollard

How disruptive is your business model? While much has been written about corporate vision, mission, process, leadership, strategy, branding and a variety of other business practices, it is the engineering of these practices to be disruptive that maximizes opportunities. Without a disruptive focus you are merely building your business model on a "me too" platform of mediocrity. Let's examine the merits of a business model that focuses on disruptive innovation as a key business driver…

Disruptive business models focus on innovation that create, disintermediate, refine, reengineer or optimize a product/service, role/function/practice, category, market, sector or industry. The most successful companies incorporate disruptive innovation into all of their business and management practices to gain distinctive competitive value propositions. "Me Too" companies fight to eek out market share in an attempt to survive while disruptive companies become category dominant brands insuring sustainability.

So why do so many established and often well managed companies struggle with disruptive innovation? Many times it is simply because companies have been doing the same things in the same ways and for the same reasons for so long that they struggle with the concept of change. My engagements with CEOs often focus on helping them to embrace change through disruptive innovation. Why didn't the railroads innovate? Why didn't Folgers recognize the retail consumer demand for coffee and develop a "Starbucks" type business model? Why didn't IBM (at one point in time considered to be the world's most innovative company) see Dell and Gateway coming? Why have American auto-makers been relegated to inferior brands when contrasted to their European and Asian counterparts? How did the brick and mortar book stores let Amazon.com come out of nowhere and get the jump on them?

Let me give you another great example…I would guess that just about everyone reading this book has at one time or another either read or at least heard of "In Search Of Excellence" authored by Tom Peters. It is among one of the best selling business books of all time whose tag line was "Lessons from Americas Best Run Companies." What most people don't know is that more than 40% of the companies profiled in the book as models for success no longer exist... You see, the CEOs of these companies that were once considered pillars of success, which are now extinct, allowed their company history to get in the way...It was in fact poor leadership that caused a failure to adapt, to innovate and to change...These so called model companies died because they were lulled to sleep by the DITWLY principle.. Did It That Way Last Year – They managed themselves right out of business...

I could go on-and-on with more examples of companies that failed to innovate but I think the point has been made. Put simply, established companies who start to play it safe, become focused on making incremental gains through process improvements and who become satisfied with their business models usually don't even see the innovators coming until it is way too late.

At one end of the spectrum take a look at the companies receiving investment from venture capital and private equity firms. On the other end of the spectrum observe virtually any category dominant brand, and you'll find companies with a disruptive focus, which are putting the proverbial squeeze on the "me too" firms occupying space in the middle of the spectrum. With the continued rapid development of technology taking the concept of globalization and turning it into hard reality facing businesses of all sizes, CEOs must examine their current business models from a disruptive perspective. Ask yourself the following questions:

1. When was the last time your business embraced change and did something innovative?
2. When was the last time you rolled-out a new product, service or solution?

3. When was the last time you entered a new market?
4. Are any of your executives thought leaders?
5. When was the last time you sought out a strategic partner to exploit a market opportunity?
6. Do you settle for just managing your employees or do you inspire them to become innovators?
7. Has your business embraced social media?
8. When was the last time your executive team brought in some new blood by recruiting a rock star?
9. Does anyone on your executive team have a coach or mentor?
10. Has anyone on your executive team attended a conference on strategy, innovation or disruption in the last year?

If you're a CEO and you can't answer yes to the majority of the questions above then your company is likely a market lagger as opposed to a market leader. If you continue to do the same things that you have always done in today's current market environment you will see your market share erode, your brand go into decline, your talent and customers jump ship and your potential never be realized. Remember the definition of insanity is continuing to do the same things while expecting different results. Bottom line; innovate, change, disrupt and prosper.

While measuring Return on Investment (ROI) is a solid business principle that helps guide corporate decisioning, I want you to shift your thinking and begin to view ROI as return on imagination, ideas and innovation. It is the return on innovation that will allow companies to maintain their competitive edge and create sustainable growth. Peter

Drucker said, "An established company which, in an age demanding innovation, is not able to innovate, is doomed to decline and extinction."

Drucker's quote mirrors my sentiments exactly...I have seen too many companies forget about the need for, and power of innovation. Without a dedicated focus on innovation it is only a matter of time until a business cannot attract or retain talent, suffers from obsolescence due to the innovation of others and watches their brand fall into decline.

Does you company suffer from the lack of innovation or does it reap the many benefits of innovation? The answer can likely be found by examining your company's organization chart...Who is in charge of innovation management? If you don't have a dedicated C-suite position focused on innovation you might really want to reevaluate your direction. While I'm not typically a fan of "title inflation" I have rarely witnessed a company with a chief strategy officer, chief innovation officer, chief imagination officer, chief idea officer, chief thinking officer, etc. who are not experiencing high velocity, sustainable growth and increases in brand equity. It is these companies who have a positive culture and who are attracting and retaining the best talent.

Let me be very clear...innovation is not the same thing as process engineering. Implementing Six Sigma or other process engineering programs to achieve short-term incremental gains in existing processes is not the same thing as adopting an innovation management approach which looks for long term gains in new areas which may require completely new business processes to be adopted. While both process engineering and innovation management are necessary and can and should overlap, they are not the same thing.

Simply open up any business magazine and look at the companies receiving the majority of the news and editorial coverage…They represent the best in innovative organizations. These companies realize the value received from innovation and choose to be market leaders as opposed to market laggers. So how do you adopt an innovation management approach for your business? Begin by considering the following recommendations:

1. Make innovation a full time initiative: Part time efforts yield part time results and even worse zero effort yields zero results. Externally hire or promote from within the best creative thinker and innovative strategist you can afford. Equip this individual with the necessary resources and watch your company grow. Nothing catalyzes growth and change like innovation.

2. Gain "active" leadership support: Innovation doesn't work in isolation. It is one thing for your executive team to talk the talk, but quite another thing to have them walk the walk. Form a "thinkubator' facilitated by your chief innovation officer and comprised of department heads, business unit leaders and other senior executives to regularly brainstorm about innovation Great ideas come from great minds and if your leadership isn't involved in the practice of innovation your business will suffer.

3. Get your head out of the sand: Remember to avoid the DITWLY (Did It That Way Last Year) syndrome. Attend trade shows, conferences, continuing education workshops and other events that expose your leadership team to the latest thinking. Hire an executive coach, bring in consultants, outsource or do whatever is necessary to drive new ideas, creative thinking and innovation.

It should be very clear by now how strongly I feel about innovation and the role it plays as a key driver in business. I am also a very big believer in the value that partnering, venturing and collaboration add as key leverage points for CEOs. Independently these two concepts (innovation and collaboration) are powerful, but couple them together and they create a catalyzing effect of unequalled proportion.

As I've described above, the "me too" era of business is gone...Following the crowd with a "herd mentality" will only run your business into the ground. From my perspective adopting the so-called "best practices" utilized by your competitors will do little more than insure mediocrity. I just finished re-reading a 64 page *"Global CEO Study"* completed by a major consulting firm in which 750 CEOs of leading companies from around the world were interviewed. The result of the survey simply confirmed what I have been evangelizing for years...Collaborate, Innovate and Dominate (my quote not theirs). At N2growth we help our clients create market dominant brands and a big part of our success formula is showing our clients the value in using collaboration to drive innovation...The bottom line is that nothing will be more meaningful to your business in the months and years ahead than your ability to excel in these two areas.

Collaboration starts internally, but in the study referenced above the CEOs surveyed also emphasized that it is essential to "defy collaboration limits" and look for collaborative opportunities outside your company spanning verticals, geographic boarders and competitive boundaries. The reality is that great ideas are rarely incubated in a vacuum. New ideas, different perspectives and creative approaches can be used to refine organic initiatives in ways that you might not ever realize if left to your own thinking.

The data in the survey clearly showed that CEOs around the globe have embraced collaboration and innovation. They understand that their success will lie in their ability to continue to add value in new ways, in new markets and with new products and services. CEO's in today's business world need to step-up and realize that they need to lead by example and drive a cultural and philosophical innovation revolution within their companies. CEOs not capable of collaborating and innovating will have a very limited shelf life moving forward. I think Kluas Kleinfeld, President and CEO of Siemens AG put it best when he said: "You can only win the *war* with ideas, not with spending cuts." The moral of this story is to avoid being caught in the innovation gap or cut off from collaborative advancements. Remember…Collaborate, Innovate and Dominate!

Much has been written about the importance of innovation but there is very little information in circulation about how to actually stimulate innovation. While most CEOs have come to accept the concept of innovation management as a legitimate business practice in theory, I have found very few organizations that have effectively integrated innovation as a core discipline and focus area.

While the old saying, "if it isn't broke, don't fix it" makes for a great sound bite it can cause irreparable harm to a company's ability to remain competitive if adopted as an operating philosophy. It is a businesses ability to use innovation to create, refine, enhance, optimize and advance all areas of the value chain that will catalyze sustainable growth. While there is always room for a great idea created through spontaneous innovation this random approach to innovation rarely works. Spontaneous innovation (what I like to call innovation by default) is at best a undisciplined and very expensive path to change. Conversely high velocity innovation (what I like to call innovation by design) occurs when supported by solid process and managed as an asset.

Since the end of the nineteenth century architects have

relied on the innovation management process pioneered by the French known as a "design charrette" to create high value, optimized solutions to design problems. Design charrettes consist of a very intense multidisciplinary approach to a brainstorming session in which design issues are assessed, analyzed, debated, conceptualized, enhanced, value engineered and planned. It is through this process that many of the world's most amazing architectural feats have been accomplished.

Much like the architect's use of design charrettes, CEOs need to adopt a process to stimulate, manage and implement innovation. The following steps outline a simple process that any business can use to effectively leverage innovation:

1. **Problem Definition and Opportunity Identification**: Using the company's vision, mission and strategy as the foundation the executive leadership needs to identify key problems, significant barriers or obstacles, critical areas of risk as well as major opportunities for which solutions need to be developed.

2. **Develop High Velocity Innovation Teams**: Based upon the assessments and objectives identified during step one outlined above, executives need to create innovation teams comprised of the right blend of skill sets, competencies and talent and charge them with development of innovation recommendations. These teams need to be comprised of both left and right brainers, new employees who have not been prejudiced, seasoned veterans as well as introverts and extraverts. Each team must have a designated leader in the form of an innovation champion with all other members of the team being equals regardless of their titles and positions.

3. **Innovation Reports**: Each innovation team should be charged with the responsibility of creating a written innovation report due within a time period certain. The

innovation report should provide the company's executive team with defined strategic recommendations to accomplish the stated objectives.

Simply following the three steps outlined above will focus your best talent on solving your most critical problems and exploiting your biggest opportunities. Innovation must be driven both from the top-down and the bottom-up. Senior leadership must make innovation a clearly communicated priority and then support the message by creating process, allocating budget, adding headcount, refocusing priorities, making changes to job descriptions and reengineering compensation plans. This type of commitment will show management and staff that the leadership is serious about innovation and will in turn encourage participation at all levels of the enterprise.

The power of innovation to totally transform a mediocre business into a category dominant company is really only deniable by the ignorant or the prejudiced. However even those businesses that embrace the concept in theoretical fashion can fail to implement productive innovation management programs if they do not understand how to measure its impact. So let's spend a bit of time on the best way to measure innovation...

There is great truth in the old axiom "you can't manage what you can't measure" and perhaps nowhere is it more applicable than as applied to the practice of innovation. Let me be clear...measuring innovation is not difficult at all if you understand it. The problem lies with the uneducated managers and executives who view innovation as a vague, ambiguous and undisciplined area that sucks time, resources and investment without demonstrable return... While the aforementioned statement couldn't be further from the truth, it is nonetheless the opinion of many uninformed people in a position of authority. They simply don't know what they don't know...

There are four CIOs in the corporate world, the Chief Information Officer, Chief Investment Officer and the Chief Innovation or Idea Officer...of the four I believe the position that a company cannot do without is the Chief Innovation or Idea Officer. As with any other important discipline your enterprise needs to place someone in charge of innovation. Without a dedicated innovation champion it is likely that your initiatives will die a slow and painful death. Furthermore, your CIO needs to be set up for success and not failure. This means that he or she must have total buy-in, both from you the CEO, as well as from other key members of the executive leadership team. Innovation must become a corporate mandate and not a corporate albatross.

Let me attempt to simplify what many strive to make complex...Innovation is simply a philosophical mindset that is used as a catalyst to accelerate growth and efficiency. It is a business driver and nothing more. However, the reason innovation is one of the most powerful business drivers is simply because it is a disruptive, high velocity, high return discipline, that can create a much greater impact than other standard business drivers.

The truth of the matter is measuring innovation is as simple as aligning your innovation initiatives with your business objectives. While innovation can be measured in many different ways, the following bullet points will give you examples to use when framing your metrics and analytics:

• **What to Measure**: Focus on measuring the things innovation is designed to impact: process, growth, differentiation and profitability.

• **Innovation as a Percentage**: Measure the trends...Look at the sales growth or contribution margin caused by products or services launched within the near term (i.e. past 18 months) as a percentage of the overall line item. The greater the influence of innovation as a growing percentage of the whole category being measured the healthier, more vibrant and sustainable your enterprise is…

- **Track Efficiency Gains**: Measure speed to market, milestone hit rates, benchmark productivity and other metrics designed to measure innovation's impact on process and efficiency.

- **Track Competitive Separation**: Measure how innovation is impacting win/loss ratios, changes in market share, increases in brand equity, competitive differentiation and other competitive metrics tied to innovation initiatives.

The bottom line is that most of the current market data indicates that companies which embrace innovation as a key business driver are the fastest growing and most profitable companies in the market. Businesses that use innovation to create, disrupt and disintermediate will attract the best talent, have higher brand loyalty and have the best chance at long-term sustainability. Don't hesitate…Collaborate, Innovate and Dominate!

Chapter 5

Talent Management for the CEO

"Mediocrity does not see higher than itself, but talent
instantly recognizes the genius"
- Sir Arthur Conan Doyle

W hen asked if I can identify the one attribute most
responsible for a company's success, one
plausible answer might be the quality of a company's
leadership. Another likely answer would be the quality of a
company's product or service. However both of the
aforementioned options (as well as just about any other
answer you could come up with) would be a natural
outcome of the correct answer…Quite simply put, the
quality of a company's talent is the single biggest
competitive value proposition a business possesses.

While there are certainly dissenting opinions on the
topic, it is my belief that quality human capital is a catalytic
asset that can be effectively leveraged across the enterprise
to generate creativity, collaboration, momentum, velocity,

89

client loyalty, a dynamic corporate culture and virtually every other positive influencing force in the corporate universe. It is quality talent that designs business models, processes and practices, understands the value of innovation, overcomes obstacles, breaks down barriers, creates growth and builds a lasting brand.

Now that I've shared my thoughts on the value of talent, let's delve into gaining an understanding of how to attract it, grow it and retain it. The answer rests in a settling for nothing less than a total and complete commitment to quality from the top down...No exceptions. There is truth in the old axiom that "quality begets quality."

Winning the war for talent begins with a company's commitment to quality leadership. Quality executive leadership will attract quality management, and quality management will in turn attract quality staff. Quality talent will produce quality process and work product which will in turn attract quality clients, investors, partners, vendors and suppliers. This quality driven value chain will produce a quality corporate culture and a lasting brand known for, you guessed it...its association to quality.

Quality is not a characteristic well served by fractionalized application. If you have a best in class compensation plan, but a low quality product offering you won't attract quality clients or quality talent. Rather you'll just attract mercenary employees looking to exploit a compensation plan and who will disappoint clients that will in turn seek solace from your competitors. The golden rule of great CEOs is that they never sacrifice quality, at any level or for any reason.

The bottom line is that a commitment to quality will position an organization such that they will have little trouble competing in the war for talent. If everything about your organization is built on the foundation of quality, your culture will largely sell itself. Moreover, if you take a values-based approach to hiring to insure that new hires do in fact have value alignment with the company, you'll cut your turnover rate measurably. My position is that it is critically important that someone want to work for you more than you want them to. If you are spending too much time selling your company it means that there is likely a value gap, your not speaking to the right individual, or the individual you're speaking to doesn't clearly understand the qualitative aspects of your organization. It is not uncommon for a values driven company built on a foundation of quality to make exceptional hires and hear things like; "I didn't think so-and-so was recruitable", or "I didn't think so-and-so would ever work for someone else again" or my personal favorite, "They must have paid a fortune to hire so-and-so".

Unfortunately recruiting talent is only part of the equation. CEOs must understand the entire talent management lifecycle in order to run a successful company. Consider that while the "war for talent" has been waged since the dawn of capitalism things aren't getting any better. In fact, with the continued advancement of technology, impending mass retirements of baby-boomers and the impact of globalization on commerce the war for talent will only continue to proliferate over time. In other words, organizations can no longer afford to assume that they will always be able to attract the talent needed to execute business strategy. Rather, it is necessary that companies be proactive and address the reality that few, if any, organizations today have an adequate supply of talent, whether it's at the executive, management or staff levels. Talent is an increasingly scarce resource...

Given that talent scarcity is impacting all businesses, it is critical to link talent strategies to business drivers which make it easier to decision how to deploy, promote, and develop talent from within to best serve the future needs of the enterprise. It is also critical to understand that business environments are shifting and that a company's talent management strategies must be adapted to current market conditions in order to remain competitive. As an example, today's talent is often virtual and/or mobile as opposed to desk bound. If you don't manage talent according to new paradigms, and take advantage of opportunities to cost effectively leverage your talent, you will not only be at a competitive disadvantage, but you will likely lose your existing talent to competitors who understand the landscape better than you...

Before you read any further I want you to stop and ask yourself the following question: How many of your employees are truly passionate about your company, its vision, its mission and the role that they play within the organization? Don't fool yourself...conduct a harsh, critical analysis and come up with a true head count of the passionate employees within your organization.

Your answer to the question above should be a very telling sign about the overall health of your business. Are people just showing-up and punching the clock to collect a paycheck, or are they personally consumed and committed to achieving the company vision? Are your employees' corporate evangelists serving as a motivating force or do they gather in small groups to gripe and complain about all the things wrong with the company and its leadership?

It is your passionate employees that are the franchise talent (regardless of position) that you should be building around. If you can't get employees to see the light and become passionate about the company and their contribution then seek to replace them as quickly as possible. Just as passion is a positive, contagious trait so are apathy and dissatisfaction. Passionate employees are productive, energized, committed and loyal assets. Apathetic employees quickly become disenfranchised liabilities that will hurt both productivity and morale. To drive home the point of how much I value passionate employees, I would take a moderately talented but passionate employee over a very talented but complacent employee eleven times out of ten...

Truly great companies are built around passionate employees. When you walk into a dynamic, thriving company you can sense the passion...you feel a certain buzz and fervor that pervades everything. Contrast this with a company that feels as if it has no pulse...If you've ever walked into an organization that feels like rigor-mortis has set in you know what I'm referring to.

As the CEO you need to understand that your employees not only want to be led, but they want to be led by a passionate leader. Ultimately they want to be passionate about what they do. In fact, they'll go to the ends of the earth because of it. Think back in history to the crews who sailed with Columbus, or the expeditioners who traveled with Lewis and Clark to explore uncharted territory. It was the passion of the leader that inspired them to take bold risks and accept dangerous challenges. While likely not risking their lives, think of the employees that started off with Gates and Allen at Microsoft, or those that worked with Phil Knight in his garage before Nike even had a name, or those employees that endured the early days with Larry Page and Sergey Brin at Google...it was their passion and commitment that helped change the landscape of business as we know it today.

To build an extraordinary company, you must light the "fire in the bellies," of your workforce...You must get them to feel passion about your organization and to connect with your vision. Passion is the essence of being a great leader…So much so that if you don't have it, you simply can't be a great leader. Think of any great leader and while you'll find varying degrees of skill sets, intellect, and ability, I challenge you to name even one that did not have passion.

The bottom line is simply this…If you don't possess an unquenchable passion for your vision, you need to recreate your vision or at least reframe your description of your vision so it becomes connected to your passion. Until you do this you will never see your company reach its full potential.

Let's turn our attention to understanding the talent management lifecycle as being comprised of the following 5 phases: 1.) Identifying; 2.) Recruiting; 3.) Deploying; 4.) Developing, and; 5.) Retaining. Furthermore, each of the 5 phases mentioned above can be broken down into subcategories. As an example *Identifying* can be broken down into definition requirements, profiling etc., *Development* can be broken down into initial training, continuing education, coaching, mentoring etc. and *Retaining* can be broken down into motivating, compensating, challenging, etc. Virtually every client I have ever served had at least some form of recruiting strategy and process in place at the time of my engagement. However, very few had processes and strategies in place for the balance of the talent management lifecycle.

While I don't mean to give the topic of recruiting short shrift as I firmly believe you should always have your hook in the water trolling for talent, recruiting is just one piece of the talent management puzzle. I believe far too much emphasis is put on recruiting and not nearly enough time is spent on the identification phase and likewise not enough attention is focused on developing, deploying and retaining the talent that has already been hired. In fact, my experience shows that most CEOs have better talent than they might think, but it is the fact that they are not developed or deployed properly that gives them a skewed perspective when it comes to assessing their own talent.

In the text that follows I will break down each phase of the talent management lifecycle so that you can begin to incorporate each of them into your company's strategy:

1. **Identifying**: The identification of talent should be a constantly occurring event. It should take place prior to beginning the recruiting process. If you haven't identified your needs/requirements and aligned them with identified solutions comprised of the skill sets, competencies, experience, and talent level you are seeking, then why even begin the recruiting process? Furthermore, it is critical that you seek to identify future leaders from within the ranks so that you can start to develop them for higher and better use activities.

2. **Recruiting**: You should hire the best talent that you can afford whose values are representative of your company and its culture. If you hire tier-one talent you'll receive tier-one results. If you hire based upon how cheaply you can bring someone aboard then you will get what you pay for.

3. **Deploying**: Looking for a sure fire way to catalyze revenue growth? Focus your best talent on your best opportunities. One of the most common mistakes that I see in companies today is that they have the wrong people doing the wrong things. When conducting employee interviews at client companies one of the most common complaints that employees' voice is that they are underutilized and not challenged. Just because someone was hired for job "x" doesn't mean that they can't or shouldn't be deployed for job "y".

4. **Developing**: Along the lines of number 3 above, if

you are not developing your talent you're wrong...A lack of talent development will not only create lost opportunity cost, but it will also eventually lead to attrition in the ranks as unappreciated talent leaves for greener pastures. Development should start on day one and never stop. New employees should be trained and mentored by more senior employees and you should consider hiring an outside coach or mentor for yourself as well as your senior executives. If you want to watch your employees achieve great things groom them for increased responsibility and develop them for greater challenges.

5. **Retaining**: If an employee was worth hiring and developing then they are certainly worth retaining. Much has been written about the exorbitant costs of employee turnover so I won't belabor the point other than to acknowledge that the costs are indeed high. I have a 4 part recipe for retaining talent and the ingredients are as follows: Motivate, Challenge, Recognize and Reward. Pay your people at the top-end of market, utilize employment contracts, deferred compensation and other forms of golden handcuffs to make sure your talent doesn't jump ship. Protect your human capital investments in order to maximize your return and manage your risk.

Bottom line...Allocate more time and attention to existing investments over new investments by operating on the bird in hand theory...If you have 90 employees and your headcount ramp calls for adding 10 new hires are you going to sacrifice the 90% for the 10%? In a properly run business it should not be an either/or situation as a good talent management plan would allow you to pay attention to both new recruits and existing employees. A focus on implementing sound talent management strategies will improve performance and morale while lowering costs and risk.

Proper assimilation of talent creates a bond of trust between the employee and the company creating a sense of loyalty that is not easily broken. Let's take a deeper dive on some of the key areas.

Recruiting: As I've discussed above I strongly suggest that you utilize values based recruiting. This doesn't just mean hire a top producer, but rather hire a quality individual that is a person of integrity and character whose values are in alignment with yours. A new hire should be someone that has invested in themselves, made good career decisions, understands why they want to be a part of your organization, is an excellent communicator and a team player. Don't hire quickly based on gut feel, but rather take time in the interviewing process to let the prospective new hire get a feel for your culture and your company. Never oversell the company, but rather disclose all the problems and weaknesses of the organization so that the new hire can make a good decision that won't be later unwound by inconsistent messaging or practices.

One of the mistakes I have witnessed CEOs make time and again is to wash their hands of talent issues in the name of delegation. While CEOs clearly cannot spend all their time on talent management initiatives, neither can they afford to just renounce their talent responsibilities and dub everything as an HR issue.

We've all experienced the let down associated with someone who slipped through the cracks of the interview process and turned out to be everything except what they represented themselves to be. The reality is that most candidates interviewing for executive level positions will have strong resumes and will handle themselves well in predictable interviewing situations. This is why it is important to put potential C-level hires through a much more demanding interview than management and staff level hires. The following three suggestions will help you spot the posers from the players:

1. **Dispense with Typical Interview Questions**: When it comes to executive level hires I tend to stray from the usual questions surrounding career history and job functions (hopefully this type of screening has been done long before a candidate reaches my office) and use questions meant to probe deeply for character, problem solving and leadership ability. I use situational questions that force them to respond quickly to the toughest of real world experiences, for which there are definitely right and wrong answers...This is a no spin zone as you either get the questions right or you don't...

2. **Conduct Interviews in Social Settings**: Get the potential hire out of the office...Take the candidate out to a ball game, to dinner, for a round of golf or any other setting where they are likely to let their guard down and reveal their authentic self. While most people can present themselves well in a controlled environment, by switching things up on them you are likely to see signs of potential issues that may surface later as problems in the workplace.

3. **Include the Spouse in the Interview**: Nothing keeps a person humble and honest like the presence of their spouse...If a candidate has embellished certain things in prior interviews you're likely to see inconsistencies pop-up in conversations held with their spouse present.

Candidates that can pass the rigor of non-traditional interviews with flying colors are likely to become valuable members of your executive team that will thrive on the demands of real world business challenges. Remember to hire slow and fire fast...This is even more important with executive level hires.

The main problem with recruiting is that in the majority of cases the wrong people are performing the function. In reality very few people actually possess the talent to identify talent. Identifying and recruiting talent requires much more than screening a resume and having a set of standard interviewing questions to guide you. There are cultural, personal, contextual and compensatory issues (among many others) that need to be addressed in the hiring process.

Just because a potential employee has succeeded in the past doesn't mean that they'll be a success for your company. Likewise, just because someone has failed in a previous position doesn't mean that they might not end-up being a top performer for your company. Assessing talent is in fact a talent in and of itself. Complicating matters further is that not all those capable of identifying talent are capable of recruiting the talent by sealing the deal...Think about it, does the person in charge of your hiring have the charisma to convince a top performer at another company to take a pay cut to work for your company?

While not every CEO should be in charge of recruiting, I also believe that if HR is solely charged with the recruiting efforts for senior management and executive level positions you'll end-up with a very weak management and leadership team. Unless your company is a large enough organization to have a Chief Talent Officer, I don't believe recruiting is an HR function (other than for administrative positions). Rather in most instances I believe HR should be a compliance, training and risk management function. It is HR's function to make sure that talent processes are implemented and followed, but having a mid-level manager attempt to identify or recruit tier-one senior talent is a recipe for disaster. The following commentary came from Steve Ballmer, CEO of Microsoft when he was asked about his philosophy on hiring:

"I did all the hiring myself for a long time. No one

joined Microsoft without my interviewing them and liking them. I made every offer, decided how much to pay them and closed the deals. I can't do that anymore, but I still invest a significant amount of time in insuring that we're recruiting the best people. You may have technology or a product that gives you an edge, but your people determine whether you develop the next winning technology or product."

I tend to be similar in positioning to Steve in that I believe one of the highest and best uses of time is to make sure that we attract the best talent for our company and our client companies. I have been either directly or indirectly involved in the hiring of well over a thousand people in my career. I can "sniff" talent a mile away and over the years I have developed a strong reputation for being able to attract people that were often considered "un-hirable." Moreover I can spot the professional interviewers and posers and can cut them out of the process early on. I must again reiterate that most people don't have this level of experience or skill and in order to insure that you make the best hiring decisions I would strongly recommend that you follow the practices listed below:

1. **Definition**: Make sure that you know exactly what you are looking for both in terms of the job description and the profile of the individual most likely to be successful in that role. If you can't define what you're looking for you shouldn't be looking.

2. **Timing**: There is wisdom in the old axiom "hire slow and fire fast." Don't panic and end-up making a regrettable hire out of perceived desperation. Give yourself plenty of runway as you will be much better-off taking your time and making a good hire rather than using the ready, fire, aim methodology and end-up terming the new hire before they eclipse their probationary period.

3. **ABH**: Always Be Hiring...Never let your organization be put behind the talent 8-ball as great talent is rarely available on a moment's notice. In the world of professional sports the search for talent often starts during the middle school years long before the potential talent being tracked by the scouts has matured. Your organization should always be on the look-out for great talent whether that talent is still in graduate school, in the military, working for competitors or working outside the industry. Some of the best hires I've made over the years were executives that I spent months, and in some cases, years developing relationships with.

4. **Identify Your Talent Scout**: Look for and identify the person within your organization that has the best nose for talent. Regardless of what position this person holds get them involved in the process. If you don't have a natural talent scout internally seek outside assistance in the form of a consultant. Don't turn your talent scout into just another corporate bottleneck, rather give them leverage by having them collaborate with outside recruiters. Outsourced recruiting is very effective and affordable if managed properly.

5. **Team Based Hiring**: While I'm not generally in favor of management by committee, hiring based upon a team approach works very well. A team consisting of your HR manager (compliance), your internal and external talent scout (the gut-check), the direct supervisor over the position being hired for (compatibility and competency) and the senior executive who is the best at selling your organization (the closer). Hiring in a team based fashion eliminates many of the typical mistakes that can be made in the hiring process.

6. **Constantly Upgrade**: I am always looking to upgrade the bottom 20% of my workforce. This can be

done through leadership development or via new hires, but at the end of the day I'm not only looking for the next superstar but I'm also looking to weed-out the under-performers as well.

Lastly, I would be remiss if I didn't discuss the role of outside recruiters as this is an often misunderstood and underutilized leverage point for CEOs. Since N2growth has a talent management practice which includes a practice group that provides both contingent and retained search services, in order to be transparent I must disclose my bias before addressing this topic. While I clearly have a strong bias favoring an outsourced recruiting model, the question merits a bit of exploration in order to provide a fair answer. In the text that follows I'll do my best to manage my bias and provide a transparent and authentic answer to a question I'm sure most of you have struggled with at some point in time...

Let me begin by providing some historical background on organizational behavior which might serve as a useful backdrop for this particular discussion. While I could go as far back as Plato's writings on the essence of leadership, Aristotle's lectures on the topic of persuasive communication or even refer to Machiavelli's work on organizational power and politics, for the sake of brevity and relevancy I'll fast forward the late 1800's in America. It was during this period of time that I believe we can find the roots of modern HR. It was during the late 1800's that industry recognized that people problems were a very real and rapidly growing concern in the workplace. It was also during this time that the US Government stepped-in to provide the first real legislative protections for the workforce.

As time has continued to march forward America has moved from the concept of "personnel administration" to "human resources administration" to "human resources management" and now we are moving on to "talent management." Nomenclature aside, the biggest challenge that HR departments face today is that of multiple and often competing agendas which in turn tends to cause staffing inefficiencies and often results in lackluster performance. As with the evolution of most functional departments in corporate America, with the passing of time has also come some empire building and title inflation. The HR department is no exception to this regrettable state of dysfunction.

Let me ask you to think about your HR department for a moment...How large is it, how big of a budget does it command and most importantly how productive is it? Upon reflection you'll find that much of your HR department is likely charged with defensive posturing associated with managing compliance and litigation risk. Other staff members are likely charged with training and administration activities, some have fallen into IT roles developing applicant tracking systems, while others perform marketing and research activities surrounding candidate development. How much of your staff is actually charged with recruiting and how senior are these people?

It is not that HR departments are incapable of making high volumes of consistently great hires, it's just that most are not organized to do so. As I mentioned earlier, if your executive level recruiting is being handled by staff level HR shame on you. Following are just a few reasons why I believe in most cases a company is better off leveraging the services of an outside recruiting firm:

1. Outsourcing allows companies to focus on core business while leveraging a broader, deeper and more senior recruiting talent pool than they

could normally afford to organically payroll.

2. When payroll costs, ad budgets, job posting fees, research costs, IT costs, lost opportunity costs, etc. are considered it is more affordable to use a recruitment firm. Why spend your budget when you can let the recruiter spend theirs?

3. There are many benefits associated with using an outside recruiting firm including realizing the benefits of a confidentiality buffer which keeps the employer in relative anonymity until they are ready to engage with a candidate.

4. Recruiting firms have existing long-term relationships with passive job seekers not readily known to most HR departments.

5. Recruiting firms have access to a wider range of candidates who may not have ever considered working in a particular industry or for a specific employer.

6. As mentioned earlier most recruiting firms are staffed with very successful senior talent as opposed to corporate recruiters who are usually less tenured.

7. Performance fees and no charge replacement guarantees make using an outside recruiter a very low risk proposition.

8. Recruiting firms have a broad array of industry trends and information which can often be useful to employers in terms of benchmarking and analytics.

Hiring is a blend of art and science and the reality is that those organizations that identify, recruit, deploy, develop and retain the best talent will be the companies who thrive in the market place.

Training and Development: Proper assimilation of a new employee during a transition to a new company is critical. In order to create a homogeneous culture and to have a continuity of messaging (both internally and externally) everyone, regardless of experience, needs to go through the same training process. Furthermore training, continuing education and development programs need to be available to encourage and stimulate professional growth and to keep an organization from falling prey to obsolescence. All new hires should have clearly defined career options and a career path with requirements and expectations being understood from the outset.

It is important to mentor not manage, and to lead rather than govern. Everyone within an organization should be assigned a mentor who can coach, troubleshoot, inspire, motivate and lead an employee toward success. Clear lines of communication throughout the enterprise will prevent miscommunication from creating unnecessary problems. Poor performance is indicative of poor leadership. If you have continuous performance problems that cannot be corrected, then what you really have is a leadership problem.

Retention is largely an issue of building a platform and culture that positions your employees for success rather than setting them up for failure. If your employees do not have the toolsets, administrative, marketing and leadership support necessary to successfully thrive in their individual role then you have set them up to fail and you won't be successful in your efforts to retain staff. A collaborative environment thrives on information sharing, business intelligence and knowledge management. If the platform isn't in place that supports these types of initiatives, then employees will look for companies that can offer such support and resources.

Deployment: One of the main keys to generating organizational leverage is for CEOs to know how, when, where and why to deploy (or redeploy) talent and resources. It has been my experience that it is much easier to recruit talent or acquire resources than it is to properly deploy talent and allocate resources.

I've heard it said that the role of a leader is to create and manage good followers. While there is an element of truth in that statement, if this is what you aspire to as a leader it constitutes a complete underutilization of leadership responsibility. I believe great leaders will mentor and coach subordinates for the purpose of identifying and developing other great leaders.

By way of example when I was in the military I witnessed many of my peers who felt it was their job to exercise command by giving orders and having complete control over their subordinates. While these individuals had all the outward appearances of running a tight ship, their units often times displayed an inability to execute at a high level in times of chaos or without frequent and direct communication with their leader. In contrast I felt it was my responsibility to use my position of influence to transfer knowledge and experience for the purpose of developing subordinates into becoming leaders in their own right. I wanted to make sure that I developed troops that could think on their feet and take charge in the worst of situations assuming that I might not be available to lead them.

Ask yourself the following questions: What are your best markets? Who are your best clients? Where are your greatest opportunities? Where are your biggest challenges? What are your biggest threats? Where are you going to deploy your top talent? Where are you going to invest your resources? Where are you going to develop more talent? Have you identified the proverbial diamonds in the rough lurking in the shadows of your organization? Where can you create more resources? If these answers are not clear in your mind it is likely that you are not getting the maximum leverage out of your talent or your resources.

It is very typical (although not very productive) to have too much talent or too much budget being wasted in areas of little or no return. Any great leader will periodically challenge his/her assumptions to test whether given the current environment they have the right mix of talent and resources applied to the right areas. If you have what is perceived as a great opportunity yet is seems to be stalled, immediately stop and evaluate the talent, resources, systems, processes, market dynamics, etc. to determine where to apply leverage to kick the initiative into high gear. By way of contrast, if an initiative has been taken from concept to implementation, and it appears to be running smoothly, you need to evaluate whether key talent and/or resources can be redeployed to other higher and better uses.

In working with a large number of very successful organizations over the years I have found that the best companies clearly understand the value, leverage, efficiency and economies of scale that are generated by assembling highly focused, motivated and productive teams. I've often said that theory without action amounts to little more than useless rhetoric, and while most companies are spinning their wheels pontificating on the merits of team building, it is the truly great organizations that put theory into practice.

Great leaders intrinsically understand that team building catalyzes collaboration, creates both disruptive and incremental innovation, facilitates a certainty of execution and is one of the key foundational elements associated with creating a dynamic corporate culture. Great CEOs deploy their talent in high-impact teams. If you are a CEO or entrepreneur and don't see team building as a priority, then the text that follows is written for you.

It is one thing to be able to recruit talent, something altogether different to properly deploy individual talent and quite another thing to have your talent play nicely and collaborate with one another. It is the responsibility of executive leadership to set the tone for great teamwork by putting forth a clearly articulated vision and then aligning every aspect of strategic and tactical decisioning with said vision. A lack of clarity, the presence of ambiguity, obviously flawed business logic or constantly shifting priorities/positions are the death of many a venture. However CEOs that implement a well thought out and clearly articulated vision create a sense of stability and a bond of trust amongst the ranks leading to a very focused, coordinated and ultimately a very passionate work environment. It is not too difficult to get your crew all oaring together when these characteristics are firmly in place.

As odd as it may sound, one of the greatest impediments to building productive teams is practicing management by consensus. While the thought that all employees should have an equal say may get some air time in business school, I have found that often the theoretical discussions that take place in halls of academia have little to do with the realities that exist in the world of business. You must also keep in mind that the classroom is one of the few remaining bastions of true equality (at least until the grades are posted).

I have been highly regarded throughout my career for building extremely effective teams and what I can share with you is that team building is not about equality at all. Rather team building is about getting various members to understand exactly what their roles are and to perform said duties with exacting precision. Building productive teams is about placing the right people in the right places at the right time and for the right reasons. Team building should have nothing to do with ego, tenure or titles but rather it should be all about collaboration and productivity. Leaders must clearly communicate to team members what their duties, roles and responsibilities are as well as setting forth a road map for performance expectations.

Team building, group dynamics, talent management, leadership development and any number of other functional areas are much more about clarity, focus, aligning expectations and defining roles than creating equality. If you examine the most effective teams in the real world you'll find numerous examples which support the thoughts being espoused in this text.

Whether you look at athletic teams, military teams, executive teams, management teams, technical teams, design teams, functional teams or any other team you'll find that the best of the best have structure, a hierarchy of leadership, a clear understanding of roles, responsibilities and expectations, clear and open lines of communication, well established decisioning protocol and many other key principals, but nowhere is equality found as a key success metric for teams.

While I'm a true believer in candor in the workplace and have always encouraged feedback and input at every level of an organization, this doesn't mean that everyone has an equal say, because they don't... Moreover, those that hold less of a vested interest, that don't have as much at risk, that don't have the experience or that may be looking-out for self interest more than the greater corporate good should not be considered equal with those that do...

While I concur that there is no "I" in team and many other statements to that effect, such statements are not meant as endorsements for management by consensus. They are simply meant to foster a spirit of cooperation. Understanding how to lead and motivate groups and teams should not be considered one in the same with creating false perceptions of equality that don't exist. Show me any team created of equals and I'll show you a team that will never reach its full potential...

Compensation, Recognition and Retention: Recognition can and should come in many varieties. Everything from fixed and variable compensation, environment, advancement/promotion, perquisites, ownership/participation, internal and external awards and exposure to a simple thank you can be key elements in the retention of employees. If your culture doesn't reward your employees for their contributions they will seek an employer who will.

As critical an issue as compensation is to a company's health and wellbeing it is not something that should be assessed solely on its own merits. Compensation is interwoven into the core of a company's culture and has many touch points across the enterprise. Moreover the best compensation plan in the world will not make up for a lack of leadership, a poor product or service offering, a lack of integrity or any number of other more important corporate characteristics and values. Taking note of the above referenced caveats, it has still been my experience that if you desire to effect change or influence culture within a corporate setting the most effective catalyst is a well engineered compensation plan. A fully integrated comp plan built upon sound underlying business logic is one of the very few strategic management tools available to an organization that can lift company morale, as well as have a simultaneous and dramatic positive impact on both the top and bottom line.

For CEOs hoping to be competitive in today's marketplace it is essential that their companies invest in processes that reward profitable behavior, align groups (i.e. teams, business units or operating entities) and meet the strategic goals of the enterprise. Realizing the direct correlation that a properly designed compensation strategy has to operational and financial performance, it is mission critical to implement an integrated compensation model that is fair, rewarding and profitable for the both the company and its employees. In order to be effective for all concerned parties, an integrated compensation plan must provide the following benefits:

- Create a better alignment between strategy, efforts and results;
- Create the proper relationship between fixed and variable compensation overhead;
- Grow revenue by quickly adapting to changing business conditions and competitive threats;
- Increase profitability by cutting administrative costs and tying compensation to variables that keep compensation overhead within industry norms while advancing business initiatives;
- Serve to focus corporate culture and behavior on revenue growth and profitability;
- Serve as a leverage point for recruiting and retention efforts;
- Create goal congruence between the employees and the company;
- Serve as a foundational catalyst for change management across the enterprise;
- Preserve continuity of equity/ownership;
- Provide long-term wealth creation for key employees without disrupting continuity or

creating a funding hardship for the enterprise;

- Maximize tax advantages for the company and its employees, and;
- Enhance the overall quality of company benefits plan by providing a wide array of meaningful benefits to employees at all levels.

Before diving in and reengineering an existing compensation plan, careful consideration should be given to both the current dynamics and future goals of the enterprise. In assessing the various options for the architecture of an integrated compensation plan the following items must be taken into account:

- The organizational and operating history of entity;
- The compensation history surrounding the entity and its employees;
- Current compensation of employees benchmarked against national standards, local competitors, current production, and future business goals;
- The duties, responsibilities and current risk exposure of employees, and;
- The employee's current and future role as team members of the company.

Let's take a look at some of the building blocks available to CEOs when considering different compensation options. The following items are all viable options to be included in a fully integrated compensation plan:

- A Competitive Salary and Benefits Program;
- Executive Perquisites (company car, use of

corporate jet, club memberships, housing allowance, expense accounts, etc.);
- Commission and Override Structures;
- Defined Benefit and Defined Contribution Plans;
- Deferred Compensation Plans;
- Incentive Stock Options (ISO's);
- Non-qualified Stock Options (NSO's);
- Employee Stock Purchase Plans (ESPP's);
- Employee Stock Ownership Plans (ESOP's);
- Phantom Stock Ownership Plans and other Non-qualified plans;
- Profit Sharing Plans;
- Bonus Pools, and;
- Project or Initiative Based Incentive and Participation Plans.

As noted above the implementation of a compensation plan in and of itself will not heal an otherwise ailing company. However, a fully integrated and well designed compensation plan, which is rolled-out in a healthy corporate culture based upon quality, integrity, and character, will have a dramatic positive result and go a long way towards dealing with retention issues.

To identify, recruit, motivate, deploy, develop and retain quality talent is not complex, but it is difficult in that it requires a significant commitment of time, money, energy and effort. It has been my experience that for many executives it is easier to complain about their current situation than to take the necessary steps to create the proper environment and culture. For those companies that are willing to make the commitment to quality you'll find no better return on investment than a thriving corporate culture comprised of talented, productive and loyal employees.

Future Trends: There has been a tremendous amount of discussion and debate in the media over the so-called "Talent Shortage" for the last few years now. We briefly touched on this subject earlier but it is important enough that we cover it in greater detail here. My question is this: Have you done anything beyond just ponder the potential consequences of this scenario? Specifically, have you taken any action either strategically or tactically to make sure that your business has the necessary talent to continue to be competitive in the market as the employment landscape changes? I believe this is a very real threat to many businesses that are not making adequate preparations...

Let's begin by looking at some of the numbers surrounding the state of the US labor force:

- The current American labor force numbers more than 76 million workers who were born between 1946 and 1964.
- Extrapolating on the demographics mentioned above, estimates are that as much as 40% of the US workforce will reach traditional retirement age by the end of this decade.
- The US Bureau of Labor Statistics estimates there will be 10 million more open positions in the United States than available workers by 2010.

On the basis of pure numerical analysis the story conveyed in the previously referenced bullet points creates a foreboding scenario for growing US companies. I have read many opinions that point to outsourcing jobs abroad as a potential solution to the talent crunch. After all, the impact of globalization on burgeoning labor pools in emerging markets such as India, China, Korea, Russia, Brazil, etc., is nothing short of phenomenal when compared to that of the US. However as is usually the case numbers only tell part of the story. The reality is that the Talent Shortage is not US centric, rather it is a truly global crisis. Just a few months ago the staffing agency Manpower Inc. released the results of a survey of more than 36,000 employers in 27 countries. It turns out that more than four out of 10 employers around the world are already having trouble hiring the right kind of staff for the right kind of money, and the problem is only getting worse. The reality is that what used to be a very large compensation gap between domestic and foreign workers is ever closing and the continuing decline in value of the US dollar is only serving to exacerbate the issue.

Let's look at India as an example...India is a country that puts almost 3 million highly educated workers into their labor force each year. India accounts for more than 65% of all IT work performed offshore producing more than 400,000 engineering graduates a year (5 times as many as the US). However demand is starting to rapidly outpace supply even in India. Consider that among just four firms (Accenture, Infosys, TCS and Microsoft) more than 100,000 jobs were added just last year in India alone. As you can see the competition for talent is already fierce and the full impact of the global talent shortage hasn't even come close to reaching its peak.

The bottom line is that companies who are not already focused on full cycle talent management initiatives will be left in the dust by more aggressive competitors as the supply of available talent continues to constrict. It is the companies that today apply serious and focused efforts toward embracing proactive talent management strategies that will be most likely to win the war for talent. If you think you can ignore the numbers outlined in this text, or that you have plenty of time and can wait until later to address the issue I believe you may be regrettably delusional in your thinking.

Chapter 6

Creating Dominant Corporate Brands

"Your brand had better be delivering something special, or it's not going to get the business"
- Warren Buffet

I am always amazed at how many otherwise savvy CEOs don't understand the importance of building significant brand equity. More to the point it amazes me how many CEOs can't even describe what a brand is. If as the CEO you have left your corporate branding to the ad agency, PR firm or your in house marketing department you are treading on very thin ice...

As with the other mission critical areas we've previously discussed, CEOs cannot relinquish their responsibility over the corporate brand. Market and/or category dominant brands don't happen by osmosis, rather they are championed and evangelized by a strong CEO who understands that branding is one of the main responsibilities of the CEO.

The truth is that most CEOs just pay lip service to branding. They don't treat the corporate brand as one of their most important assets rather they just let it evolve or evaporate as the case may be...The reason for this as I mentioned above is that most CEOs really just don't understand the value and advantage that creating sustainable increases in brand equity affords their company.

Is the practice of branding an art form that only the ethereal creative types that lurk in the shadows of ad agencies understand or is branding a business process based on a formulaic approach to managing success metrics across the enterprise and throughout the value chain?

The question posed above, if asked of any group of corporate executives and marketing professionals, would be guaranteed to spawn a fierce debate. However the outcome of the debate would likely produce no clear answers other than identifying people's natural bias. The best way to validate the preceding statement is to select a handful of employees from different departments that have varying levels of authority and responsibility from within your business, ask them to informally audit your brand and see for yourself what the result is.

What usually happens as a result of this exercise is that some members of your focus group won't even understand (much less be able to define) the difference between marketing, sales, PR, advertising and branding. Others will believe that building a strong brand lies solely in mastering one of the aforementioned disciplines to the exclusion of the others. You'll find that some of the group will feel that the answer to a strong brand will be found in reengineering your corporate identity, ad campaigns, packaging or other forms of external creative. While other participants will think it is simply a matter of creating more distribution channels, expanding your sales force or utilizing more mediums to penetrate new markets. By the end of the conversation the finance representative in the group will likely form the opinion that you have a brand in decline and would be an advocate of implementing an immediate decrease in MarComm expenditures.

The truth of the matter is that creating a powerful brand requires a blending of art and science...the confluence of creative efforts along with solid business process combined with patience, courage, great strategic vision and excellent tactical implementation. Even further complicating the matter is that the path one chooses to travel in building their brand should be uniquely evaluated and engineered based upon the individual characteristics of their business, product or service, depth and breadth of market, the competitive landscape, the depth of their human and financial capital and a myriad of other influencing factors. It is precisely a result of this level of complexity that you find very few market dominant brands worldwide.

Is your organization building a growing, sustainable brand on the road to category recognition or dominance, or is your brand stagnant or in decline and viewed as just another MarComm buzzword that is a leftover thought, missing agenda item or even worse, ignored all together? Your brand can be one of your greatest corporate assets if managed soundly. If given short shrift, or ignored, a non-existent brand or brand in decline can also become one of your most significant corporate liabilities. In fact the choices made (or not made) by an executive team with regard to brand management can impact the human capital talent hired and retained, the attitude and culture of the corporate environment, corporate valuation, consumer opinion, velocity of growth, the ability to influence vendors and suppliers and a litany of other major influencing factors on your corporate health.

A BRAND DEFINED

So, let's start looking at what a brand is not: A brand is not a name, a logo, a product or a service... These are examples of brand assets, associations, and extensions that should be considered in the creation of your brand architecture and the development of your brand components. However, they are clearly not brands in and of themselves.

So what is a brand? A brand quite simply is a collection of perceptions in the mind of your stakeholders. It is the image that your employees, shareholders, customers, partners, vendors, the media etc. have when they think, touch, feel or otherwise interact with your company. It is the mixture of attributes, tangible and intangible, which if managed properly creates action, value and influence.

Now that we've defined what a brand is, let's turn our attention to how you properly conceive and build a brand. The following items are individual brand components which when put together in a coordinated fashion are the brand:

Brand Vision: Great brands are not built without great vision. CEOs must take ownership over and develop a sound brand vision. Not only must the brand vision be sound, it must be in alignment with the corporate mission and it must be communicated with clarity and continuity across the enterprise.

Building a powerful brand will only happen if executive leadership is completely committed to building brand equity as a key strategic objective. Executive teams often spend time on strategic planning and vision creation as it relates to virtually every other aspect of their business. However this is not always true with regard to branding. Any time spent on brand vision and brand strategy will produce significant returns on brand equity.

If as the CEO you don't know what your brand vision is how can you possibly communicate to anyone else how you want them to think of your brand? Your brand vision is the nucleus of your brand. It supports, authenticates and validates why you are in business and where your business is headed. It defines your brand graphics, brand language and brand voice. It serves as the guidepost for all decisioning related to brand.

Brand Management: Creating brand equity is best accomplished through proactive and aggressive brand management that focuses on creating vision and goal alignment throughout the entire corporate value chain. While a brand should be managed as any other corporate asset, it is critical to guard against the conventional perspective that values traditional tangible assets more highly than intangible assets such as sound business intelligence or the competitive talent advantage of a sales force; the bias that accounts for every postage stamp, paper clip and stapler, but discounts a company's image and reputation in the market.

All organizations should make the creation of brand equity a priority and allocate dedicated human resources to brand management to insure that outcome. Whether your organization has legions of brand managers or doesn't even have that position on the org chart, every company needs a brand champion. The entire culture needs to adopt the mentality that brand building is mission critical to the overall sustainability of the enterprise.

Brand Measurement: The trusted management axiom that states: "if you can't measure it you can't manage it" is never more accurate than when applied to brand measurement. How do you tell whether or not you are building a dominant brand? You measure it…

Resist the temptation to focus on tangible, easily

quantified assets when establishing your measurement metrics and gauging your success. It is all too common for companies to measure what is easily identified and reported rather than what is critical to long term success. An example of this would be that it is much easier to focus on volume rather than market penetration or quarterly revenue growth over the measurement of customer satisfaction, or the size of the average sale vs. the lifecycle value of a client relationship. When an enterprise focuses on hitting quarterly revenue goals regardless of the impact on brand equity, the result achieved will be the result deserved...systemic long-term destruction of the corporate brand.

Brand Research: In today's "age of information" there is no reason to be uninformed. Virtually anything can be assessed, analyzed and segmented. There are in fact very few barriers to receiving access to both a large *quantity* and/or high *quality* of information. That being said, even with the plethora of analytics available many companies seem to have a lack of understanding of the value of quality research and therefore don't avail themselves to its many benefits. On the other side of the spectrum there are organizations that are tantamount to information junkies who do everything possible to corner the market on being informed only to spawn a culture of "analysis paralysis." The solution: focus on actionable brand research...

Actionable brand research is the art and science of turning metrics into decisions. It has often been said that "knowledge is power", but I believe that true power lies in the application of knowledge resulting in action. Findings that lead to conclusions without action may be informative but will not lead to profit.

Too many businesses start to believe their own corporate mantra over time whether or not it is accurate. Be cautious of a corporate culture created by default rather than by design. If your vision, mission, strategy, tactics and processes are not founded on actionable research that is underpinned by solid business logic you may find yourself rapidly approaching the proverbial brick wall while never seeing it coming until you crash into it. If your brand research is non-existent, aging, non-actionable or it's been a while since your brand assumptions have been challenged, it's time to restate all your questions and question all your answers.

Naming Conventions: Whether it's your corporate name, domain name, or the name of your product, service or intellectual property, a brand's most valuable asset can in some cases be the name itself. For instance, a name can have inherent selling power when the word(s) or symbol(s) stand for something by highlighting the value, usefulness, uniqueness, power, sophistication, competitive positioning or any other definable value proposition. By this measure, for example, "Excedrin Migraine" is more valuable, more descriptive, than "Advil," and "Weight Watchers" promises more than "Jenny Craig."

However the value of the "name" itself is substantially less important when contrasted with the market dominant power of those brands which have created brand equity after decades of smart, creative and consistent brand-building activities. "Sierra Mist" or "Mellow Yellow" for example, no matter how descriptive and colorful, can't approach the brand equity of "Seven Up," a heritage built on decades of smart, innovative, creative ad spending and marketing campaigns. Any brand analysis or audit should give tremendous weight to the use or misuse of a name. Investigating the practical limits of line extensions, for example, forces us to distinguish between those new product efforts that re-invest brand equity and those that dilute it.

Brand Content: Content is king…Brand content by my definition includes all forms of external messaging which can include reports, proposals, PR, corporate identity pieces, ad creative, all forms of media, packaging and virtually anything that externally messages your brand.

Whether your market is B2C, B2B or B2B2C your brand content will impact the entire customer relationship management lifecycle. Content will often constitute a first impression in the form of advertising or website content, validate a first impression with follow-up sales collateral, serve as an influencing factor in key decisioning in the form of proposal content or become the final communiqué with the end-user in the form of packaging.

Effective brand content is creative, sticky, synergistic, defining, distinguishing, effective, targeted, powerful and appealing. Furthermore it will also have an impact by creating a desired action or reaction. The leverage gained from good brand content can often times be substantial. The difference between mediocre brand content and great brand content can be a key item in the difference between a sustainable brand as contrasted with a brand in decline.

Brand Reach and Frequency: When most people think of advertising effectiveness, they tend to think in terms of the size of their ad budget. While spending is clearly important, it is only one of several influencing factors and certainly not as important as reach, frequency, or content. In today's competitive marketplace the few remaining mass markets are dominated by very large established brands and are in turn virtually impossible to penetrate for new up and coming brands. Niche markets on the other hand seem to be created almost daily. Given this competitive and complex market it is best to think of reach, frequency and content as related but separate assets in your brand portfolio.

Given the current market dynamics stated above reach has been elevated over frequency in terms of its effectiveness in recent years. However with the proliferation of new marketing tactics and the corresponding toolsets that target narrowly focused segments there are now efficient, cost effective methods to penetrate specific consumer affinity groups and psychographic slices of the ever shrinking mass market.

Brand Consistency and Coordination: Consistency from year-to-year, as well as consistency across all mediums, markets and channels serves as the fundamental cornerstone of good brand management. Frequent rebranding comes not only at a very high price, but if a brand changes its image too often, it runs the risk of having no image at all. It should be noted that a strong commitment to brand must be strongly protected and adhered to otherwise only a few years into any brand-building campaign the agents of change-for-the-sake-of-change will lobby for rebranding or repositioning.

As important as brand consistency is, brand coordination may be equally if not more important. Managing multiple vendor relationships such as ad agencies, promotion organizations, packaging companies and PR firms is fraught with peril. A CEO striving for brand consistency is likely to suffer from a nervous breakdown from the chaos associated with attempting to achieve a seamless and synergistic execution from people who aren't reading from the same script. It is not at all unusual for vendors to have their own agenda each pursuing their own vision which in turn loses the singular focus that consumers demand, and as the CEO you should be striving for.

Brand Public Relations: An often overlooked tool in

the brand management arsenal is PR. Great timing and sense of market opens up opportunities for editorial and news coverage, which is essentially unpaid advertising with a kicker...the kicker being that PR has more credibility than paid advertising. Clearly defined, strategically focused public relations can be a powerful tool. It's an asset that can enhance brand image and build brand equity... if it is consistent with other messages.

Brand Likeability, Respect & Power: If your brand is likable, then the market is much more likely (no pun intended) to embrace your message. It's a fundamental truth: people buy from brands they like. However don't confuse brand likeability with brand respect or brand power. While likeable brands can be respected or powerful brands these attributes are clearly not a given. Consider Microsoft: one of the world's most powerful brands, respected by many, but liked by very few. Contrast Microsoft with Google...Google is well liked (perhaps less so than in recent years), well respected and very powerful. If you manage your brand well enough to secure the holy grail of branding and achieve this trifecta you will find yourself breathing rarified air.

Brand Positioning: This is the specific niche in which the brand defines itself as occupying within the competitive environment. Positioning addresses differentiating brand attributes, benefits and segments. Brand positioning is what establishes emotive connections. It creates reasons to buy, engenders loyalty and causes internal and external stakeholders to advocate for your brand. An improperly positioned brand is a brand being wasted.

Brand Target: This is an assessment of which constituencies you want your brand to influence. Your brand target should be comprised of all industries, sectors, verticals, micro-verticals, groups, associations, audiences, companies and individuals that you want your brand to reach.

Brand Performance: Perceived performance is a key factor in a buyer's initial decision to purchase and actual performance is a key factor in the decision to repurchase. Several aspects of brand image can weigh in on influencing a consumer's perceptions of anticipated or perceived performance. Major contributors to perceived performance are ad campaigns, PR, promotions, your sales force, your website, packaging, etc... anything and everything that promotes a brand to consumers.

Companies that have worked so hard to build a brand often stand idly by while the brand falls into decline because they became comfortable with so called "Brand Loyalty". This has the unintended consequence of allowing your customer base to be taken for granted. It is not recommended that any enterprise rely on the blind loyalty of people who have chosen a brand in the past to continue to do so in the future. Brand owners should focus on earning the loyalty of their customers, not just assume because they've earned it in the past that it will continue on in perpetuity. Consumers only purchase and repurchase brands that continue to live up to their perceptions of added value.

Brand Identity: Your brand identity should be developed based upon your brand vision, positioning and target. Your brand identity is the outward expression or manifestation of the brand. The brand's identity is its fundamental means of consumer recognition. This would include your naming, logo, taglines, graphics, voice, collateral packaging, advertising content and language.

Brand Promise: This is the brand's essence expressed in the simplest, most single-minded terms. For example, Volvo = Safety or Disney = Entertainment...The most powerful brand promises are rooted in a fundamental customer need.

Brand Experience: These are the feelings and emotions tied to an interaction with the brand that influence the perception of whether your company is fulfilling your brand promise. It could come from a display in a retail environment, the purchase or use of products and services, the impression created by advertising, journalistic commentary or public opinion. A positive brand experience will increase customer satisfaction and loyalty whereas a negative brand experience will have the inverse affect.

Brand Personality: This is the attribution of human personality traits (trust, warmth, humor, imagination, etc.) to a brand as a method for achieving differentiation. This is usually accomplished by consistent, long-term, advertising, marketing and public relations.

Brand Continuity: Ensuring that all products/services in a particular brand range have a consistent name, visual identity and positioning across geographies, mediums and markets.

Brand Protection: Creating competitive barriers to entry for those intending to encroach on your brand is essential. Furthermore it is necessary to be willing to enforce those who violate the intellectual property rights associated with your brand. This is the implementation of strategies and tactics (both market and legal) to reduce the risk and liability from the effects attributable to counterfeiting, diversion, tampering and theft so that differentiating thoughts and feelings about the brand are maintained.

Brand Value: Proper assessment of the demand side pull from the market, competitive positioning, margin requirements, market segmentation and a variety of other factors will help you determine where you should position your brand in the value chain. Not all brands command a premium as some brands have to fight just to maintain price parity, while others must take a low cost discount approach to the market.

If your brand can establish and maintain a value-added premium price versus the competition, you can feel honored that your brand is perceived as a value-added brand. However keep in mind that positioning alone does not determine value as brands at every level of the value chain can achieve brand equity and dominance.

Assuming that you have deep pockets and a lot of patience, growing a recognized brand isn't difficult...spend heavily across all mediums with consistent, creative, on message advertising while simultaneously conducting an aggressive public relations campaign. Avoid controversy, maintain a high likeability factor, be a business of character that engenders trust and confidence on the part of your target market(s), produce a quality product or service at a competitive price point and provide great customer service.

The description above paints the perfect illustration of why branding is one of my favorite topics...It is complex. While the illustration above is true in every sense, unless you are a very large enterprise it is unlikely that you have the time, money, staffing or external professional relationships to execute a brand management strategy such as the one outlined above.

So what's the best way to build a brand if you're not a Fortune 500 company? Be very, very smart...Unfortunately I'm not kidding. If your business isn't one of the deep pocketed companies capable of executing a strategy like the one mentioned above then you must understand how to cost effectively appropriate and deploy resources and talent, as well as apply leverage, velocity and economies of scale to your particular company and its corresponding market in a manner that still produces results. The simple truth of the matter is that building brand equity with limited resources is one of the most difficult things to accomplish in the business world.

The following items constitute the basic tenants of branding, which if incorporated into your brand management strategy will help build a solid brand regardless of the size of your company or your ad budget:

1. Treat your brand as an asset not an afterthought... If building brand equity is not a key strategic focus for your executive team then don't be surprised if your brand remains in stealth mode;

2. Never sacrifice quality... Your products, services, leadership, management, culture, customer service, communication, etc. must all reflect high standards of quality. Quality equals value in the eyes of the consumer and as a result often corresponds into justifying price premiums;

3. Know your market...make sure you understand the needs and desires of your customers/clients and do everything possible to satisfy them.

4. Understand the competition... Creating competitive separation is a must. Without a clearly recognized competitive value proposition your brand will be forced into the commodity market of competing on price point alone.

5. Choose the right mediums... If you don't have the luxury of being able to spend across mediums select the medium that will give the most frequency and reach at the lowest cost. Put simply spend your money where you get the biggest bang for the buck, and;

6. Be consistent... Consistency in all things throughout the value chain is mission critical for CEOs. Continuity should flow from vision to mission to strategy, to tactics to process.

Mixed messaging or practices has killed many a brand.

We've gone in depth on defining branding, but now I want to spend some time looking at the value associated with strong brands. Assessing a brand's value is not rocket science, nor does it constitute ethereal hocus-pocus. Good brands have real value and understanding this is central to measuring whether or not your brand equity is increasing or whether you have a brand in decline. As a CEO or entrepreneur measuring the brand value of the enterprise you must value your brand in order to understand and manage your brand. In the text that follows I'll give my perspective on not only why a brand should be valued, but also how it should be valued...

Think about this... If you can't place a value on a brand how do you determine how much to invest in it, how do you measure its success, and how do you raise capital for it? If you can't calculate a tangible value associated with your brand it is time to have a conversation with your CFO. By the time a finance officer has reached the C-suite he or she needs to have a solid understanding of how to apply and leverage, finance and accounting principles to the benefit of all business units aggregating value for the benefit of the entire enterprise. Not understanding the value of a brand, much less how to value it is absolutely unconscionable...

Understanding the key to measuring brand equity is central to maximizing valuation. In fact, brand equity can actually represent a large component of a company's total valuation. This is specifically backed-up by research from Zyman Institute of Brand Science which notes that brand equity can actually account for more than 60% of total valuation when using Tobin's Q ratio. This ratio is a valuation methodology devised by John Tobin of Yale University, Noble laureate in economics. Even if you

don't believe Tobin's academic hypothesis, all you have
to do is look at the absolute value placed on real-world
brands...At the time of this book was going to press
Google's brand was valued in excess of $80 billion dollars
and there are easily in excess of a few hundred brands that
sport economic value of more than $1 billion dollars
including BMW, McDonalds, Goldman Sachs and the
like. Even smaller privately held companies with
valuations of $10 million or less can experience brand
equity that accounts for a considerable portion of their
worth.

The four standard brand valuation methodologies which
are accepted by both the Financial and Accounting
Standards Board and the International Accounting
Standards Board are income-based, market-based, cost-
based and hybrid valuations. While there can be reasons to
use one methodology vs. another it has been my experience
that using the hybrid model to capture the best benefits of
each of the other three methodologies often results in the
highest overall valuation.

The fact of the matter is that real brands have real value
and produce real returns. I want to encourage readers not to
conduct a brand valuation just for the purposes of
retroactive scorekeeping, but rather to understand how
brand equity is driving overall financial performance so
that you can make better business decisions.

The text above provided a fairly in depth overview of
both how to calculate a brand's value as well as describing
why it is critically important to focus on creating brand
equity. However nothing illustrates the impact of a brand's
contribution to the overall health of a company more than
an assessment of its financial contribution marked by its
valuation, its change in growth and its short-term
momentum. In that vein I thought it would be interesting to

peel back the layers of some of the best and worst performing brands in order to validate proof of the mission critical nature and value of a brand...

I would strongly recommend that you read BrandZ, which is an annual study of the world's top 100 brands (by valuation) conducted by Millward Brown. The beauty of this report is that regardless of how you feel about the business logic used or the key metrics evaluated in their analysis, it was nonetheless objectively applied across all companies covered in the study. The study breaks down brands by category and does a decent job at profiling sector analyses as they relate to brand growth. However for our purposes here I simply want to use the data contained in the report to validate what I've been saying for as long as I can recall...Brands matter.

Pulling from Millward Brown's study, in the lists below I've highlighted a comparison between the 10 most valuable brands, the 10 fastest growing brands, and the 10 brands in greatest decline:

Top 10 Most Valued Brands (by market value of brand equity – note: the figures contained below fluctuate with the market and likely have changed since this book was published)

1. Google - $80+BB
2. GE - $61.8BB
3. Microsoft - $54.9BB
4. Coca Cola - $44.1BB
5. China Mobile - $41.1BB
6. Marlboro - $39.1BB
7. Wal-Mart - $36.8BB
8. Citi - $33.7BB
9. IBM - $33.5BB
10. Toyota - $33.4BB

10 Fastest Growing Brands (percentage increase in valuation over 1 year)

1. Marks & Spencer +135%
2. Best Buy +113%
3. Target +88%
4. Google +77%
5. ABN Amro +72%
6. Apple +55%
7. Gucci +49
8. Starbucks +45%
9. Hermes +44%
10. Cingular Wireless +39% (now AT&T wireless)

10 Brands in Greatest Decline (percentage decline in valuation over 1 year)

1. Home Depot -33%
2. T-Mobile -32%
3. Dell -24%
4. Intel -23%
5. Budweiser -15%
6. Vodafone -12%
7. Microsoft -11%
8. Cisco & Chevrolet -10%
9. Ford -9%
10. IBM & Goldman Sachs -7%

Let's begin by contrasting Google and Microsoft...Microsoft once thought of as an impermeable brand that would play king of the mountain forever vs. Google, the dominant brand of this decade. When you consider that Microsoft fell from the number 1 position last year to the number 3 position this year suffering an 11%

decline in valuation, while Google saw a meteoric rise to the most valuable brand in the world increasing its brand equity by 77% this year it provides strong testimony to the linkage between vision, strategy, operations and brand.

In even the most cursory review of the above three lists (not to mention if you take the time to read the entire report) you can see how brand affects value. Witnessing former blue chip brands such as IBM, Goldman Sachs, Dell, Intel and Home Depot fall into decline shows the need to carefully manage a company's brand. Declining brand equity not only erodes overall corporate valuation, but it also impacts customer loyalty and crushes revenue growth.

If as a CEO reading this book you don't fully understand that brand equity and momentum are perhaps the most critical success metrics to be measured and managed then your personal reputation and brand is bound to decline as rapidly as the corporate brand you have failed to steward.

As I've said before, real brands have real value…in fact recent studies confirm what many of us have known for quite some time, which is that brand equity can become one of the largest assets on a companies balance sheet and ultimately lead to increased valuations. To illustrate this point I'm going to look at brands (as opposed to companies) as potential acquisition targets…

Brands that have been well engineered have also been heavily invested in creating both tangible and intangible worth which makes them solid acquisition targets. It is much easier to acquire a stand alone brand than create one from scratch as you are leveraging the investments of time, money and the collective efforts of the previous brand owner. Even if a brand is not particularly well known or even if it happens to be dormant there may still be significant logic to acquiring the brand. Moreover acquiring the right brand can give you immediate access to certain markets and demographic as well as pave the way for geographic expansion.

By decoupling a brand from the operating entity that owns it, your acquisition will likely be void of much of the brain damage typically associated with the post acquisition integration efforts of rolling-up a going concern (employees, infrastructure, etc.). By stripping the brand out as a stand alone asset you acquire the brand equity which will often include significant good will, mindshare, marketshare and any number of other benefits in a much less complicated transaction that can close in a short period of time. Lastly, many companies undervalue their brands (especially if they are not currently active) and will often times divest themselves of a brand at a discount over true market value. This is in stark contrast to a company's perception of their own enterprise value which they almost always value at a steep premium.

While the text above discusses brand acquisition from the buy-side perspective the logic should not be lost upon potential sell-side players. Those companies that have developed brands (active, dormant or somewhere in between) looking to leverage their investment should look into a valuation of their brand assets and consider the possible divestiture of brands that don't fit into the company's operating strategy going forward and where it makes economic sense to do so...

In conclusion, branding is a subject that all CEOs must become fluent in. The custodial responsibility that goes along with championing and stewarding your company's brand is not optional if you're serious about your job as CEO. Not only is building a rapidly growing and sustainable corporate brand both exciting and challenging, but it is also financially rewarding.

Chapter 7

Process...The CEOs Most Undervalued Asset

"The key to great process is surrender, not control"
- Mike Myatt

As my quote above reflects, I believe all great CEOs must not only understand the need to implement processes, tools and systems to leverage better results, but they must also surrender to being process driven. I know that the topic of process doesn't thrill anyone, however as unattractive as this topic is on the surface, it can sometimes be a defining difference between success and a lack thereof. In this chapter I'm going to focus on only four things: The value of process, organizational theory, customer experience, and knowledge management.

Process...even the word itself has come to hold a negative connotation for many CEOs. With the plethora of conflicting information that has been written about process management and process engineering combined with the nightmares we have all experienced as a result of bad process, many CEOs fear the pain associated with flawed process more than they value the benefits created by good process. While process is overly discussed and receives a lot of attention, it is rarely seen by CEOs as a strategic asset to be leveraged. Rather most CEOs tend to think of process as a mid-level management tool and they therefore miss significant opportunities because of a blind spot resulting from flawed thinking.

One of the ways successful companies gain a competitive advantage in today's market is through the implementation of sophisticated, efficient and effective process. Business processes serve as the central nervous system for your organization providing a framework for every action, decision, activity or innovation to flow from and through. There are many who would say process stifles creativity and slows production…While I would concur that this statement is usually the case with bad process, nothing could be further from the truth as it relates to good process. Good process serves as a catalyst for innovation, which in turn optimizes and accelerates workflow and enhances the productivity of business initiatives.

Understanding what constitutes bad process is the first step in recognizing how to avoid business process pitfalls that plague many companies. Let's start by examining the three main misconceptions related to process:

1. Process is not a new software program or application. While toolsets can enhance process or can become a by-product of process, they do not in and of themselves constitute process. Don't get caught in the trap of perpetual spending or development as a solution, but recognize that if you're caught in this trap that it is a symptom of bad process not a reflection of good process.

2. Process is not a "Band-Aid" fix. Good process is not reactionary. A series of bubble gum and bailing wire

solutions put in place in haste as a knee-jerk reaction to the latest problem is not good process design. Process by default will never provide the benefits of good process engineering by design.

3. Process is not a panacea. While good process will help optimize any business it will not make up for shortcomings in other disciplines or functional areas. Process is not the main driver in business but a critical support system built for enablement, delivery, accountability and measurement.

Good process comes as a by-product of clarity of purpose. It is the natural extension of vision, mission, strategy, objectives and tactics. It is in fact working down through the aforementioned hierarchy that allows process to be engineered by design to support mission critical initiatives. Recognition of the fact that you don't start with process design, but rather you finish with process design is critical to the development of good process. Process is the part of the value chain that holds everything together and brings an ordered, programmatic discipline to your business.

Good process results in a highly usable infrastructure being adopted across the enterprise because it is efficient for staff and provides visibility and accountably for management all of which increases the certainty of execution. Good process across all areas of the enterprise will result in elimination of redundancy and inefficiency, shortening of cycle times, better knowledge management and business intelligence, increased customer satisfaction, and increased margins.

I encourage you to not let apathy, negative experience based upon results of bad process or flawed implementations, or the fear of complexity keep you from benefiting from the numerous advantages created by good process engineering. I would also strongly encourage you to evaluate all of your current processes so that you can discard or reengineer bad process and improve upon good process, striving for excellence in process design. Great CEOs understand the value of great process…Do you?

The best thing about well conceived process outside of the fact that it provides for an increased certainty of execution is that it provides the CEO with solid analytics that can be used to constantly refine performance. The reality is that each industry, sector, vertical and micro vertical have unique business drivers. Furthermore depending on how a business is positioned, where it is in its maturation lifecycle or what its current financial condition looks like will dictate which factors may be most important to measure.

As a CEO the key to instituting sound processes is to develop a culture of project management. You should break everything down and view it as if it was a project. Projects have a beginning, middle and an end…they have benchmarks and deadlines which are tied to budgets and they have human accountability for delivery. As the chief executive the more you can view business as a project the more efficient and successful both you and your company will become.

Great process not only enables and supports, but it also measures and analyzes. One of the key benefits of well conceived processes and systems is that they provide visibility to key data points which can be assessed and refined. In this section I'll provide you with an overview of some general guidelines that will be useful to any CEO attempting to define and analyze success metrics. I believe that most measurements can be broken down into the following 5 categories:

1. Static Historical Measurements;
2. Quantitative Return Measurements;
3. Qualitative Return Measurements;
4. Quantitative Performance Measurements, and;
5. Qualitative Performance Measurements.

It has been my experience that most businesses at least attempt to measure items 1 and 4, but often times fail to measure the other 3 categories, which also happen to be the most meaningful measurements. The most successful companies measure all 5 categories (as well as various subsets) with their focus being on items 3 and 5.

Let's begin by stating what should be the obvious...All businesses need to monitor the basic static financial measurements of revenue, expenses, breakeven, earnings and cash flow. While analyzing these drivers will give you some basic operating information and should be measured by all businesses, they are also somewhat myopic. The reason I say this is that while historical analysis is important, it is taking the next step of using these historical measurements as baselines to calculate forward looking return drivers that will help you as the CEO fine tune your business.

Quantitative Return drivers such as Return on Assets (ROA), Return on Equity (ROE), Return on Investment (ROI), Return on Cash (cash-on-cash), and Return on Human Capital (ROHC) calculations will give you more useful information than the static calculations mentioned above. The great thing about return analysis is that each area can be broken down into several more refined qualitative return calculations.

Examples of qualitative return analysis might be Return on Marketing (ROM) which is a qualitative measure of marketing expenditures and investments. Another example would be Return on Innovation which would be the qualitative measure of the contribution impact on new ideas and initiatives. These types of qualitative return drivers allow you to make forward looking investment decisions that can have immediate impact to the business.

Examples of Quantitative Performance Measurements would be items like revenue hurdles, billable time, production hurdles and service levels. These are the metrics of how an organization performs against its benchmarks.

Implementing Qualitative Performance Measurements are where an organization truly becomes productive in its analytics. These sets of metrics focus on the measurements surrounding things that develop talent, build teams, manage the customer experience, improve customer satisfaction and increase brand equity. Getting to the qualitative level of performance measurement is difficult in that it is often necessary to overcome a set of traditional leadership behaviors and beliefs.

Ask yourself this question…do you measure the metrics that are critically important or just the ones that are obvious and easy to measure? If company leadership can make the attitudinal adjustments necessary to create accountability and focus on qualitative performance metrics they will find that it is these measurements that help to catalyze growth, enable execution and create dynamic organizations.

Let's turn our attention to the process of creating a sound organizational structure for your company. Great CEOs have well functioning organizations and understand their role in creating a healthy corporate culture. Well conceived organizational construction is built upon the four pillars of functional, political, environmental and social considerations. Organizational theory is a hot topic these days getting a decent amount of attention. However the reality is that most CEOs create complex structures that create more barriers than they remove.

Over the years I've seen every type of org chart in existence. Some have come and gone only to come again. Every year or two the latest revolutionary thinking in corporate organizational theory spawns a new form of charting. The dynamics of corporate organization are so revered by B-school professors and management consultants that an entire generation of corporate management has drunk the org chart Kool-Aid. CEOs often rush to adopt the latest thinking without any consideration for whether or not the new form of structure is even appropriate for their business. So powerful is this dynamic that entire companies and numerous products have been built to support these latest trends. In the time it has taken to write this section of the book it wouldn't surprise me if Visio had a new product release (Okay, I'm stretching a bit).

So, is an org chart a corporate asset or a waste of time? The answer depends on the purpose behind its creation, the process used to create it and the corporate purpose for the existence of the chart post creation. The following list contains my top 10 reasons not to create an organizational chart:

1. To give the CEO an opportunity to view his name at the top;
2. Because you need to beef up your management presentation and you have room for an extra PowerPoint slide;
3. Your management consultant told you to create one;
4. The business planning software you purchased has a template for one;
5. Your CFO just read a new article on corporate

organizational theory;

6. You just attended an off-site where someone drew an off-the-cuff chart on a dry erase board and it looked good;
7. When reviewing your competitor's website you noticed they had one and your website needed updating anyway;
8. There wasn't anything better for the intern to do;
9. Someone got a promotion, and;
10. It just seems like you should have one.

Putting the satire aside, a business should in fact have an organization chart. A sincerely motivated, properly constructed and actively implemented organizational chart can in fact help refine the operational aspects of any business. The development of an org chart should be a serious initiative born out of solid underlying business logic, process and methodology. Culture and environment are considerations that are often times completely ignored in the design of and org chart while perhaps representing the most critical architectural elements. It is important for CEOs to look well beyond titles and examine where the real spheres of influence reside within an organization so that they can be effectively engineered into the organization to avoid bottlenecks and create leverage.

The most common mistake made by executive leadership is that the organization chart is created way too early in the process before business rules and logic are aligned. Much like the order of operation principles that apply to an algebraic formula, if you get the sequencing wrong you can't solve the problem. An org chart is not where you start the process, but is rather the culmination of many processes helping to insure a certainty of execution and clarity of direction by creating a roadmap to be followed.

There's an old joke in business circles that says "every company has two org charts...the one that's put into graphical form and incorporated in the business plan and the one that never gets published but is actually representative of how things really work." The process of corporate organization is most succinctly and easily understood by recognizing that the org chart should enter the organizational construction cycle as deep into the cycle as possible to avoid the joke that led off this paragraph. By not creating your organizational paradigm too soon there is a clear picture of who, what, when, where, why and how. It is only at this stage that you can properly align expectations, with process, culture and environment.

The bottom line is that I have observed all types of organizational structures (in vogue, antiquated and otherwise) succeed and I have also seen them fail. It is not the "type" or the "style" of chart used that works or doesn't, rather it is the process of design that was used in creating the org chart that will determine its usefulness, functionality and adoption. As CEO it is your responsibility to insure that your organizational structure reflects alignment with your corporate values and vision such that you have the right people deployed on the right initiatives for the right reasons. If you get this one right your position of chief executive will not cause nearly the amount of stress that it will if you get this one wrong.

We've addressed in earlier sections of this book the need for CEOs to be externally focused. I can't communicate how important it is that as the chief executive you let your current and potential customers serve as your conscience. If you innovate around customer needs, fulfill your brand promise and keep your customers satisfied, they'll reward you with increased customer satisfaction and loyalty. That is why it is critical for CEOs to focus on measuring the customer experience.

As many of you know, I am a huge fan of well conceived Customer Relationship Management (CRM) initiatives. That being said, I have rarely seen CRM implemented to its full potential. Most companies can claim an element of success in some aspect of CRM proficiency such as sales force automation, database marketing, development of a knowledgebase, etc., but the reality is that most companies absolutely miss the boat in harnessing the true power of CRM which is improving the customer experience. I want to spend some time addressing a critical area you should be focused on as a CEO which is Customer Experience Management (CEM)...

Before I go any further let's get the semantical arguments out of the way...Some will claim that a well conceived CRM initiative includes CEM as a subset. Others will claim that CEM is a stand alone practice differing measurably from CRM, and I actually believe that CEM should drive CRM functions such that CRM is actually a subset of CEM. The initial concept behind CRM was to integrate experience with management...Oddly enough I have found that most business people use CRM and CEM inconsistently or worse yet interchangeably...a very big and very costly mistake.

Now that you're totally confused let me see if I can clear things up a bit...My belief is that experience has been unknowingly, but nonetheless systematically bled out of CRM over the years by operationally focused bean counter types who tend to focus on measuring incomplete and certainly less meaningful data points to begin with. In short, most CRM practitioners have traditionally assumed an internal (inside-out), operationally centric approach to customer management and strategy. CRM purists (those who really get it) or CEM practitioners differentiate themselves by assuming an external (outside in) approach that focuses on customer centricity.

While many companies tout their CRM initiatives and pride themselves as being customer centric, the reality is their efforts are woefully inadequate. This is because most CRM platforms measure customer interactions solely upon product purchase history, preferences and satisfaction. As should be obvious this set of metrics is biased not only to product centric data, but also toward historical data and does not take into account experience or forward looking trends and preferences. CEM focused platforms measure experience data not just product data and focus much of the efforting on forward looking analytics. Misguided CRM practitioners focus on selling more product while true customer centrists who display a bias toward CEM focus on closing the gap between a company's brand promise and the delivered customer experience which has the same resultant impact of increasing sales. However the revenue increases that come as a result of CEM tend to be more profitable and sustainable than those achieved via CRM.

Just as a mountain climber can choose different routes to the summit, companies can likewise choose different approaches and focus points in how they manage the customer relationship and experience. However as the mountaineer's choice can influence time, degree of difficulty and the eventual success or failure of the climb, so will a company's choice between a historical product based platform (CRM) vs. a forward looking experience based platform (CEM) influence their degree of success or failure.

Let's pivot quickly and discuss the value of knowledge and information to the CEO and to the overall enterprise.

147

One of great challenges for any business is to learn to efficiently and cost effectively leverage knowledge on an enterprise wide basis. We have all heard the saying that "knowledge is power"...we've all also heard the refinement of that saying which states that "the application of knowledge is power". I prefer to take it one step further and say that "the successful application of knowledge at the right time, for the right reasons and with the proper emphasis results in a certainty of execution that creates power." In the text that follows I'll provide you with some insights that will help you to not only leverage your knowledge to increase returns, but also will help address how to protect your knowledge to mitigate risk.

Let's begin by defining knowledge management (KM)...While this alone may spur fierce debate, for simplicity sake I'll define knowledge management as: "an organization's ability to collect and convert data into information, turn information into knowledge and knowledge into an operating advantage." The operational advantage created through effective KM should allow an enterprise to effectively address current needs as well as to strategically drive innovation and forward planning.

Put more simply, a corporation's employees must be able to acquire knowledge (learning), transfer knowledge (out of the head and into an information system), apply knowledge (from the information system into an actionable event), manage knowledge (execute with focus, timing and precision), and secure knowledge (keep it from evaporating or even worse from walking out the door to a competitor). Let's see if we can bring this issue a bit closer to home for some of you...Ask yourself the following questions:

- Have you ever had a disruption in business continuity because someone who possessed a wealth of experience and/or information retired, quit or was terminated?

- Have you ever lost a deal or had a major operational problem because somewhere in your organization the right hand didn't know what the left hand was doing?
- Have you ever found yourself in the unenviable position of desiring to terminate an employee only to be held hostage by the fear of losing the knowledge that they possess?

While I could go on ad-nauseum with day-to-day operating examples of how a lack of KM discipline can adversely affect a business I think I've probably dredged-up enough painful memories for now. Let's turn our attention to the following 3 practices/concepts that can immediately be used to implement a KM system for your business:

1. **KM is more about people than systems**: In order for KM to flourish in a corporate environment the business must value data, information, business intelligence, research and other forms of knowledge as a strategic corporate asset. Furthermore KM must be recognized as one of the core elements of your corporate culture. Encourage and reward the public sharing of knowledge and education.

2. **While KM is more about people and culture than systems, you still need a system**: Start with developing standard naming conventions, file protocols, nomenclature and other heterogeneous standards that put everyone on the same system. By requiring everyone to work on the same platform and environment and within the same toolsets a certain sense of continuity and community is developed. Develop a mantra of "document, document

and when in doubt, document" and make this as painless as possible. There is an old technology axiom that states "usability drives adoptability". Whatever toolset you select must be easy to use so that it is viewed by employees as something that makes their job easier, not more difficult. That being said, there is a plethora of add water and mix intranet and KM solutions that are affordable and easy to use.

3. **Protect your corporate knowledge**: All employees should sign work for hire, non-disclosure, non-compete and non-circumvention agreements that make sure that all knowledge developed will remain corporate knowledge. Furthermore make it a practice to utilize copyrights, service marks, trademarks, license agreements, patents and other intellectual property protections to protect the corporate investment into knowledge assets.

The bottom line is that you can harness disparate elements of data and information and convert them into corporate knowledge assets to create a sustainable competitive advantage, or you can choose to sit back and conduct business as usual…The choice is yours.

Chapter 8

Secret Weapons of Great CEOs

"There is no greatness without a passion to be great."
— Anthony Robbins

In this chapter I'll discuss what most of you have always wondered about but were never taught...The simple reality is that legendary CEOs possess a few secret weapons that their less successful counterparts don't. This operating deficit that most CEOs struggle with happens in some cases due to an element of naiveté, but in most cases it happens as a result of ignorance (there is a big difference between the two). Naïve CEOs are the chief executives who are simply operating with a few blind spots due to inexperience. Ignorant CEOs already believe that they know everything, need no help and can do everything on their own.

SECRET WEAPON NUMBER 1: PLAYING TO WIN

"You must play boldly to win"
- Arnold Palmer

Great CEOs play to win...This particular message is not one that will please the politically correct as I'm not going to talk about competing rather I'm going to address the topic of winning...Want to succeed? It's easier than you might think...just don't quit. My first football coach used to say: "Don't even bother showing up if you're not going to play to win..." Mind you I tend to be a bit competitive, but even so, that phrase has stuck with me my entire life. I don't often bother with taking on an endeavor unless I plan to accomplish the task at hand and that means not quitting until I meet the objective. It is that "refuse to lose" and "never say die" attitude that I picked-up on the playing field and had further reinforced during my time in the military that provides me with a competitive advantage. I may not be the smartest, the most talented or the luckiest person, but I guarantee you that I am the hardest working individual you've ever come across.

I have found that dedication, determination, attention to detail, commitment and focus are the traits that have been most valuable to me throughout the years and are therefore the strengths that I tend to play to. The good news is this...if you examine the aforementioned traits you'll quickly see that I possess no special skill and I have no secret tricks up my sleeve. Rather the things that have allowed me to serve my clients well are things that anyone can harness and leverage if they have one thing...the desire to do so.

I could certainly paint a more complex picture of what it takes to be successful by citing esoteric management theories, but the truth of the matter is that I just don't quit until I get the job done. I don't spend my time complaining about the challenges and obstacles, rather I spend my time solving problems and creating solutions. If my objective is to get to the other side of the wall I don't really care if I go over the wall, under the wall, around the wall or through the wall...I just care that I get to the other side. While I might spend a bit of time evaluating the most efficient strategy for getting to the other side of said wall, it will ultimately be my focus on the tactical execution of conquering the challenge that will determine my success. A bias toward action is always a better path than falling prey to analysis paralysis.

I once played an entire half of a football game with a fractured ankle, early on in my first entrepreneurial venture I found myself at a critical nexus and chose to liquidate personal assets to meet payroll, I've gone as many as 4 days in a row without sleeping to stay the course and solve a critical issue, I've helped to create wealth and opportunity for my clients, I've led teams to achieve things that others said couldn't be accomplished, I've kept my family a priority having raised two wonderful children and having been married for 23 years and the list could go on...My point in describing these actions is not to pat myself on the back for anyone could have done these things, but the reality is that most people don't. They choose to accept defeat...they don't play to win...They aren't willing to do what it takes to be successful...They quit.

Part of playing to win is learning to develop the heart of a warrior. I have come to believe the same characteristics that are present in the heart of a warrior are also present in the most successful CEOs. Regardless of whether or not they have served in the military, today's CEOs would be well served to possess the characteristics of a warrior in their pursuit to achieve sustainable growth and long-term success. Commitment, attention to detail, discipline, service above self, honor, integrity, perseverance, the ability to both lead and follow, to execute with precision and the ability to adapt, improvise and overcome are all traits that will serve you well in the boardroom.

There are many so-called management gurus in today's politically correct world who would take great exception to what I'm what I'm espousing in this section. They would tell you that the classic strong leadership traits that define our nation's best military leaders are outdated and they don't display a proper amount of empathy and compassion. I'm here to tell you that strength and compassion are not mutually exclusive terms…rather the strongest leaders are in fact the most compassionate leaders. When I was in the service my troops slept before I did, they ate before I did and they were cared for before I was. A leader's greatest responsibility is not for his/her own glory, but it is for the well being of those whose care has been entrusted to said leader.

The characteristics mentioned above will allow you to inspire and lead with a focus and commitment not present in DNA of those leaders who don't have the heart, mind and soul of a warrior. It is the ability to stay mentally focused on achieving the mission at hand regardless of circumstances that will help you take your organization to that next level.

A warrior's heart has served my family well in both business and life in general. It is the mental agility, a fierce determination and a never say die attitude that has carried us through the best of times and the worst of times. My father was a Marine before he was an attorney, I served in the Army before I entered the business world and my son is currently attending the University of Virginia on an Air

Force ROTC scholarship. While not all great business leaders have served in the military those of you who possess the heart of a warrior understand the advantages you derive from your military bearing, command presence and state of mind. I've rarely come across students of military history that don't have a great command of both strategic thinking and tactical implementation.

I strongly recommend to all CEOs that they learn to develop a command presence and lead from a committed and passionate position of strength. The word "passion" comes from a Latin root which means quite literally to suffer. If you're passionate about something it means you care so much that it hurts...Playing to win, refusing to surrender and having the ability to make the tough decision or the needed sacrifice will allow your company to continue taking ground and will keep the competitive advantage on the side of your enterprise.

SECRET WEAPON NUMBER 2: A PERSONAL CEO ADVISOR

"If a man coaches himself, then he has only himself to blame when he is beaten"
- Roger Bannister

The second secret weapon of great CEOs is that they have a personal CEO advisor on retainer who is loyal to only them and who is constantly operating behind the scenes on their behalf. Often times it is through the use of a CEO advisor that the barrier of self is conquered. This strategic advisor is similar in function to a political advisor, sports agent or chief of staff. Jack Welch, Meg Whitman, Bill Gates, Michael Dell and a whole host of other successful CEOs have reaped the benefits of using a CEO advisor.

The truth of the matter is that CEOs simply have more to gain from intelligent counsel than any other person on the org chart. Given the nature of the position along with the numerous studies that have been authored which provide ample data affirming the extraordinary results that can be achieved by utilizing a CEO coach, I'm always amazed at the number of CEOs who don't yet have a coach on retainer. In this section I'll examine the reasons why I believe all (yes I said all) CEOs should have a coach or advisor.

As bright, talented, experienced, motivated and savvy as most CEOs are, they are only one person...Moreover CEOs are the individual in the company most likely to be operating in a vacuum. The only thing CEOs can count on is that their performance is constantly being evaluated by virtually everyone in the value chain. Combine that with the fact that performance standards and expectations are constantly being raised and it is no wonder that CEOs often feel overwhelmed. The reality is that in today's competitive business world a CEO is only as good as his/her last decision, or their ability to stay ahead of contemporaries and competitors.

As the CEO the reality is that you have no true peers within the business, so where do you turn for advice and counsel? If you're like many CEOs you turn to your subordinates...This is not where you should seek unbiased information as it is unlikely that your subordinates will tell you the hard truths or provide you with open candid criticism of your actions. They are certainly not in a position to hold you accountable or most times even provide you with intellectually challenging input.

Most successful CEOs make heavy investments in

building their skill sets, knowledge base and subject matter expertise early in their careers only to make minimal investments in their professional development when they reach the C-suite. It is however at the C-suite level that an executive must be on top of his/her game as they have the broadest sphere of influence, the largest ability to impact a business and they also now have the most at risk...It is at this place that the CEO should make the heaviest investment in refining their game because it is at the chief executive level that increased performance will pay the biggest dividends.

Wouldn't it be nice to seek counsel from an objective third party who has walked in your shoes and is not caught-up in office politics therefore having no axe to grind or turf to protect...someone who has an extensive network outside your business and is a true intellectual and experiential peer of yours? The right CEO coach can afford all these benefits and more...

In addition to my operating duties at N2growth I also maintain an active personal advisory practice where I provide counsel to a select group of CEOs and entrepreneurs. For most of these professionals the decision to retain my services was driven by one of two distinct motivations. Some of my clients had a defensive motive in that they wanted to protect what they had worked so hard to achieve while others had an offensive motive in that they were looking to take their companies or careers to the next level...Regardless of which camp they fell into these were already very successful people who recognized that its lonely at the top and that they could not afford to keep operating in a vacuum. I actually have a few clients where I am just one member of a coaching team that is on call to deliver real time advice and assistance when the need arises.

I don't actually like the term coach as a descriptor for what I do as that particular label can tend to give the wrong impression. Sure, in some cases I coach or mentor, but most of my clients simply view me as their closest personal advisor. As their advisor my role is to serve them in the manner that will be of greatest value whether it be behind the scenes or in plain view. Over the years I have played the role of ambassador, emissary, influencer, facilitator, expediter, personal brand manager, lobbyist, buffer/shield, crisis manager, negotiator, publicist, strategist, tactician, collaborative thinker and a variety of other roles as needed. I am on call 24/7/365 and have been known to fly around the globe at a moments notice if an event merits such action or attention on my part. Bottom line…I make things happen and I get things done at the behest of my clients for the purpose of enhancing or protecting their personal and professional brand or enabling the accomplishment of anything ranging from a single task to a lifelong goal. These are the traits you want to look for in a coach, and if you desire the best results I urge you not to settle for anything less than the best advisor available.

If you are not consistently working on improving you will eventually hit a plateau and the only way to break through the plateaus that will inevitably arise is to continually improve upon your abilities and to further develop your talent. Let's say for sake of argument that you are indeed the best at what you do. Does this mean that there is no room for improvement and that you should not seek the help and counsel of others?

Let's use Tiger Woods as an example…At the time of this writing (and quite probably for sometime to come) he is without question the most dominant golfer on the PGA tour. Yet he still has a coach, frequently practices improving his game and has a team of professionals surrounding him with the goal of increasing his level of performance. He is already considered great, but is constantly working to improve his competitive capability in order to build upon what he has achieved and to sustain greatness as opposed to fall from greatness.

The trick for CEOs who desire to transition from being successful to becoming significant is to get out of your bubble and get honest with yourself. It is not necessary to succumb to the bondage of self...Find a CEO advisor who can credibly assess your strengths and weaknesses, understand your goals and help you see the things that you cannot see yourself, that others won't tell you, or even if they do tell you that you refuse to acknowledge. Step outside yourself and begin the journey from being successful to becoming significant.

The question is not whether a CEO advisor will provide results...It is rather can you find the right advisor capable of producing the results you're looking for? Let me issue an open challenge: I can come-up with a virtually endless amount of legitimate reasons and benefits for why you should have a CEO advisor on retainer and I'll bet you can't come-up with a single valid reason (excuses are not reasons and don't count) why you shouldn't...

SECRET WEAPON NUMBER 3: A STRONG PERSONAL BRAND

"Branding is everything. A young girl once came up to me and told me I could be famous because I looked just like Richard Branson!"
- Richard Branson

After reading the chapter on branding I hope you now

possess a very clear understanding of the need to build brand equity at the corporate level or for products, services, intellectual property, etc., but now I want to turn your attention to secret weapon number 3 which is developing a strong personal brand. The truth is that most CEOs completely miss out on one of the most powerful strategies for creating professional leverage...the creation of their own personal brand.

When reading newspapers and periodicals, listening to media interviews on the radio, watching guest appearances on the TV and seeing who gets the speaking invitations you'll notice that it is usually those CEOs who have positioned themselves as innovators and thought leaders through a carefully managed personal branding campaign. These individuals may, or may not, have anything more to offer than their peers other than the fact that they knew how to brand themselves as subject matter experts.

Picture a very successful high profile company in your mind and you will likely find that their executives have not only established themselves as leaders inside their firms, but they are also perceived as industry heavy weights and power brokers to the external world. When a company's senior executives are viewed as subject matter experts and leaders outside of the company it makes them more valuable to the company. It is a true win-win scenario in that the executive who knows how to manage his/her brand equity in turn increases the brand equity of the enterprise. Because the corporation benefits from the executives ability to brand themselves, they are willing to pay more for their services and work harder to retain their talent.

Regardless of how you feel about the following list of individuals you must agree that they have done a remarkable job of building a personal brand which has often times resulted in the creation of modern day empires.

Think of Warren Buffet, Oprah Winfrey, Donald Trump, Bill Gates, Michael Dell, Sam Walton, Ted Turner, Richard Branson, Steve Jobs and a whole host of others and you'll quickly see just how powerful a strong personal brand can be. In fact spend some time browsing through the Forbes 400 and you find that you recognize far more names than not...View a list of the Fortune 500 CEO's and you'll be surprised how many of their names have been converted into strong personal brands. Look at the Inc. 500 or Entrepreneur Hot 100 lists and you'll see a number of strong personal brands in the making.

The reality is that most of us will probably never achieve the status of icons, nor do most of us really aspire to that end. However increasing your personal brand equity is good for adding value to your company's brand, leveraging your earning power and improving your job security and/or marketability. Personal branding is far more than an ego-play; it is smart business. If you don't know how to create a strong personal brand the following tips will start you in the right direction:

1. Make those around you successful. While some personal brands are built at the expense of others, or on the backs of others, the most highly regarded personal brands are built on the success they have created for others. Think "selfless" as opposed to "selfish."

2. Hire a CEO Coach. This is something that many successful CEOs struggle with as their pride can be a barrier to seeking the wisdom and counsel of others. However this is one of the single best investments you can make in building a powerful, sustainable and respectable personal brand.

3. Invest in continuing education: Okay, so you already earn a substantial income, run your own (or someone else's) business and you're busy...The sad fact is that it is far easier to reach the C-suite than to remain there. You will only stay in the corner office if you continue to refine and advance your skill sets and competencies. Never sacrifice or forego learning because you think you don't have time or worse because you think you already know it all.

4. Learn to work the media, or hire someone to do it for you. When it comes to the media you only have three choices: a.) you can try and remain invisible, but anonymity won't help you build a brand; b.) you can be a target for the media and while controversy is not always a bad thing it causes more unnecessary brain damage than you will likely want to incur, or; c.) you can be a friend of the media and serve as a subject matter expert who is available as a resource for the media…While the choice is yours, I'd personally recommend option C.

My advice is simple…find a good CEO advisor and start building your personal brand strategy yesterday…you'll be glad you did.

SECRET WEAPON NUMBER 4: BECOMING A GREAT FACILITATOR

"He who has learned to disagree without being disagreeable has discovered the most valuable secret"
- Robert Easterbrook

Are you a great negotiator? To be considered a savvy negotiator is to be held in high esteem in the world of business and in some circles is worn as a proud badge of honor. If you possess a reputation as a shrewd negotiator you are feared in the board room as an adversary to be reckoned with. While many a consultant, author and trainer have made personal fortunes teaching the finer points of negotiation, it is my belief that if you find yourself negotiating you have already missed the boat. I'll share with you in the text that follows why negotiation is inherently flawed as a business practice...

I don't consider myself a great negotiator. I do however consider myself to be an excellent facilitator who attempts at all costs never to negotiate. Great CEOs don't negotiate they facilitate...As I stated in the opening paragraph if you find yourself negotiating you've already lost. Negotiating is not an art to be mastered rather it is a sloppy approach to be avoided. If you find yourself negotiating you will find yourself posturing, spinning, manipulating, being slick and even deceitful. Negotiation by its nature is a zero-sum game (my gain is your loss). In other words the goal at the outset of a negotiation is to benefit from someone else's loss which I find to be an unacceptable premise for doing business.

Sure there are those who say that win-win scenarios are altruistic fantasies that don't exist, but I'm here to tell you that all good deals are in fact win-win scenarios. Negotiation is adversarial and I'm all about expanding relationships and spheres of influence not creating enemies. When I've wrapped-up a deal with someone I want them to be excited about doing business with me again in the future and not regretting the day we met. When I hear someone reminisce about the great deal they just negotiated all I can think of is will the deal stick and even if it does get traction what about the bad taste left in the mouth of the other party. While it may seem tempting to exploit the immediacy of a situation or circumstance the long-term consequences of such actions are detrimental to your reputation and credibility.

My clients don't hire me to stick-it to someone, but

rather to facilitate a desirable outcome that achieves a stated objective while reflecting well on their brand and adding value for all concerned parties. So, if you don't negotiate what do you do? Don't negotiate facilitate…Look to create opportunities for others, to add-value, to align interests, to understand needs, to facilitate, enable, educate and to inform. Don't be lazy and trick somebody just because you're smart and you can…rather be a professional, do your homework and help people attain their goals and objectives. It is more fun, more rewarding and definitely more profitable…

SECRET WEAPON NUMBER 5: A STRONG AND ACTIVE NETWORK

"More business decisions occur over lunch and dinner than at any other time, yet no MBA courses are given on the subject."
- Peter Drucker

As a CEO nothing is more valuable than the quality of your relationships. Whether you realize it or not your success in business (and in life in general) will largely be dependant upon your ability to not only establish key relationships, but in your ability to leverage, influence and add value to your relationships. We have all known professionals that have been smarter, more affable, better looking, possess a better CV or are more talented yet they never seem to rise to the top. These professionals that seem to have the whole package yet can't reach the brass ring have failed to understand the power of relationships. Even more regrettable is the person who has the rolodex to die for who doesn't do anything with it. In the text that follows

I'll discuss how to build a powerful sphere of influence.

Let me begin by defining what I like to call the relationship value chain. We all have a personal network, but as I'm sure you've come to realize many people within your network are for lack of better definition inactive contacts or acquaintances. The majority of people in your network are people that while known to you are not perceived to be high value contacts and you therefore don't invest yourself heavily in building relationships among that group. Moving up the food chain from inactive contacts you'll find your active contacts are perceived to be of higher value such that you have taken the time and investment to build a relationship. Then at the top of the food chain are your power contacts. These contacts comprise the contacts that can create influence, open doors and generally make things happen. I actually prefer the term personal sphere of influence over network as it is a more action oriented descriptor and helps to keep me focused.

Lest you think I'm overly mercenary in my approach and only view people as pawns in a chess game let me introduce you to Myatt's golden rule of relationship management: "Give, give, give some more, give until it hurts and then when you have nothing left to give, you guessed it...give even more". The best relationships are built by helping others succeed. It is through assisting others in reaching their goals and objectives that you will find success. Reflect back upon your own experience and contrast the responses you've received when you ask for help from someone that you've previously provided assistance to vs. asking the same favor from a casual acquaintance that you've never lifted a finger to help.

Generally speaking there are two types of spheres of influence...those that just evolve over time by default and those that are strategically engineered. I have spent years developing relationships spanning geographies, industries and practice areas that I have invested both time and money developing to a high level of mutual benefit. People in my network benefit from my active pursuit of helping them achieve their objectives and I in turn benefit from their reciprocal treatment. Don't confuse a database with a sphere of influence. A database consists of information records and a sphere of influence consists of meaningful relationships…a point of distinction lost upon many.

In addition to my operating duties at N2growth I maintain a small consulting practice in which I serve as the closest personal advisor to a select group of CEOs and entrepreneurs. You're probably saying to yourself "what does this guy know about networking? He only runs a small consulting practice." Fair question…What you may not know is that I've developed an active network of 50,000+ relationships in order to serve my clients and associates. I have built a reputation that I can reach just about anyone with a few phone calls and do it with credibility and influence. My reputation is therefore synonymous with the quality of my network for I am usually retained to accomplish what others have failed to do based upon the influence of my network. My network is my business.

The problem is that most CEOs even if they intellectually understand the benefits of what I'm espousing just don't do the work it takes to build a powerful network. Great networks take great amounts of effort. Think of the most successful people you've ever known and they will always seem to know the right person to call on in any given situation to influence or decision the needed outcome. This type of influence doesn't just happen, rather it has taken years of painstaking effort. If you want to create a powerful sphere of influence start by taking the following five steps:

1. Take pause and examine where you are currently in your professional career as contrasted with where you want to go. Think about the people who could help you reach your destination more quickly and efficiently. Don't put any artificial ceilings on your thinking...If knowing Richard Branson, Bill Gates, Michael Dell, etc. would be of benefit take note of this and remember that almost anyone on the planet is only a few degrees of separation away from you.

2. Once you have a clear vision of where you want to go take a personal inventory of your contact database. See who it is that you know, but also pay attention to who they know. Review in detail each and every contact in your database and rank them on a scale from 1 to 5 with 5 being the contacts perceived to be of the greatest value to you. Make a detailed relationship plan for each of your contacts that rank 3 or higher. Take a personal interest in rekindling those relationships and finding out how you can help them succeed.

3. Develop a strong core competency and then give freely of your time and knowledge. Be visible and accessible and don't approach business solely based on a "what's in it for me" attitude. Don't be a joiner unless you can be a contributor. I belong to a number of organizations that I will likely never see a paying client from, but it is through these groups that I build relationships and connections that will help me serve my clients. These relationships are built upon the back of the time I invest in them. Relationships don't get built overnight and are not built without active participation.

4. Your network is your business...The core value of your business is not actually steeped in the conventional thinking imparted to you in business school. The reality is

that the true intrinsic value of a business is in the network that adds value to your products, services, brand, stakeholders etc. A strong network equals sustainability in that it is your network that will provide you much needed resources and leverage in both good times and bad.

5. Don't waste time with those that only see problems and flaws, but cannot ever seem to create solutions. The world is full of bitter people, small thinkers, naysayers and those that just get their kicks out of sniping from a safe distance. Remove these people from your network. Associate with energy gainers and not energy drainers.

While without question valuable and no doubt integral parts of your personal arsenal your biggest assets are not your personal brand, your talent, your keen intellect, your charisma, your character or other commonly thought of personal strengths or attributes. Rather your largest personal asset is the collective value of the relationships you possess...

SECRET WEAPON NUMBER 6: BREAKING THROUGH THE BARRIER OF SELF

"Strip away the excuses, rationalizations and justifications and the only thing standing between you and whatever your objective may be is what you see staring back at you when you look in the mirror each morning."

- Mike Myatt

This fifth secret weapon of Great CEOs is that they know how to blow through self imposed barriers. How rough are your edges? Which aspects of your professional life need to be smoothed, polished, developed or refined?

Do you understand what it takes to close the gap between success and true greatness as it applies to you? We have all known truly talented executives and entrepreneurs who while successful still have a huge barrier precluding them from reaching their full potential...themselves. In this section I'll discuss how to break through the final obstacle between success and greatness which is most often the barrier of self.

Over the years I have come to believe that the professional talent curve is comprised of a range consisting of the low-end, mid-point, upper-end and several points in-between. Under achievers are those professionals whose talent and ability far exceeds their level of performance. Achievers are those who perform up to their ability and the over achievers are the rare few whose performance consistently eclipses their natural ability. The professionals at the upper-end of the talent curve have learned to grow beyond self imposed boundaries and have developed their skill sets and competencies to levels that most never thought them capable of.

I can't tell you how many successful professionals I've met that have lost key employees, failed to close substantial transactions or missed significant opportunities, had clients consciously make a decision to work with other less talented practitioners or inferior companies simply because they were tired of the attitude/ego/arrogance, had their company hit a plateau or any number of other tragic and avoidable circumstances simply because they were either unwilling or incapable of recognizing their own shortcomings. They were capable of doing what was necessary to polish the rough edges and take their game to the next level, but for whatever reason chose not to.

Okay, so you're the CEO, you own your own company or run someone else's, have had your fair share of media attention and industry accolades, have achieved many of your goals and earn a better living than most...The bigger questions are:

- Are you successful or are you a true success? Do you know the difference?
- Are you content and do you really feel successful or are you frustrated that you haven't reached your full potential?
- Have you truly maximized your potential, or do you even recognize what that is?
- Are you making others successful and do others view you as a true success?
- How do you know what you don't know?

The difference between being successful and being a true success is to bridge the gap between being good and becoming great. I believe it was Shakespeare who said "Be not afraid of greatness; some are born great, some achieve greatness and others have greatness thrust upon them." Whether greatness is inherited, earned or stumbled upon it cannot be sustained without consistent effort to refine and develop your skills and abilities. A cavalier reliance upon what has worked in the past will only take you so far. It is very common to watch professionals leverage intellect, aggressiveness, creativity, innate leadership ability, charisma or other positive traits to become successful. However it is uncommon to see professionals take those same characteristics and truly develop them to the extent of achieving greatness.

I am a big believer that there is truth in the statement "that a person can be too smart for their own good." How many times have you witnessed a very bright person fail to solve a problem that a younger, less experienced and perhaps even a less intelligent person solved with seemingly little effort? While raw intelligence is a valuable commodity, in-and-of-itself and to the exclusion of other traits and characteristics, the sole reliance on IQ can be a barrier to professional growth and maturity.

Is your intellect standing in the way of your success? Are you so enamored with how smart you are that you can't get anything done? In the text that follows I'll share the keys to leveraging your intellectual assets as opposed to having your intelligence serve as a barrier to your success...

By nature of what I do for a living I tend to work with very bright people. It has been my observation that hyper-intelligent people can tend to think themselves into trouble and out of opportunities with great ease...Whenever I find myself discussing issues of intellect, ego, leadership etc. I'm always reminded of the poster that you see from time-to-time displayed in someone's office which reads: "Rule number one: the boss is always right. Rule number two: When in doubt refer to rule number one." If you find yourself rationalizing or justifying positions based solely upon intellectual reasoning without regard to practical realities, timing or other contextual considerations you may be too smart for your own good. Just as a lack of belief in gravity won't prevent you from tripping, simply believing a particular opinion or theory to be fact doesn't mean your right.

Often times the problem with intelligent people lies simply in the fact that they have come to enjoy being right. Bright people can quickly find themselves in the position of confusing ego with intellect and can sometimes defend ideas to the death rather than admit they're wrong. This confusion of ego and intellect often stems from bright people successfully arguing wrong positions over time such that they've built their persona around being right, and will therefore defend their perfect record of invented righteousness to the death. Smart people often fall into the trap of preferring to be right even if it's based in delusion.

So how do you know when you've crossed over to the dark-side and can't tell the difference between fact and fiction? The following items will help you discern whether or not you are using your intellect properly or whether you've just simply bought-off on your own propaganda...

1. Consistent Conflict: Do you find yourself in a perpetual state of debate? Do you find yourself thinking "why am I the only one that gets it?" Is it more important for you to be right than to arrive at the correct resolution to an issue, problem or opportunity? Are you known as a bitter, pessimistic or negative person? If any of these issues describe situations that hit too close to home then you may want to take a step back and do some self-evaluation.

2. Exclusivity vs. Inclusivity: Do you use your intelligence to intimidate and stifle others or to encourage, inspire and motivate others? Do you wonder why you can't seem to retain tier one talent or why you lose key clients? If your brilliance is polarizing as opposed to serving as a magnet which attracts then how smart are you really?

3. True Success: If an independent third party came into your business and interviewed your peers and subordinates alike what would that feedback look like? Do others see you as successful or are you merely a legend in your own mind? What I think of myself is not nearly as important as what my family, friends, clients and co-workers think of me. If those you surround yourself with don't hold you in high regard then you have no reason to.

The bottom line is this...the gift of intellect is an asset to be thankful for and put to good and productive use. It is not an excuse to be lazy, arrogant, mean-spirited or delusional. Don't let your intellect stand in your way, but rather use it as an asset to develop those around you to their full potential thereby increasing your chances for long-term success.

SECRET WEAPON NUMBER 7: GREAT CEOS FOCUS ON PRODUCTIVITY

"Productivity is never an accident. It is always the result of a commitment to excellence, intelligent planning and focused effort."

- Paul Meyer

Great CEOs understand the importance of maximizing productivity. Let's face it, productivity is the standard by which most of us are judged in the business world. At the end of the day, in most business environments your destiny is likely to come down to a "what have you done for me lately" type of evaluation. My question to you is this…Are you as productive as you think you are, or even as productive as you used to be? Would your co-workers agree with your assessment? I want to share my thoughts and experiences about any number of different things that can adversely affect your ability to produce, as well as some of the key items that can leverage your ability to optimize productivity.

Has the speed at which business is transacted in the 21st Century completely overwhelmed you? Do you find yourself flirting with disaster by constantly brushing up against deadlines? Are your work hours increasing without a corresponding increase in income or satisfaction? Do you wish you had more time in a day? If you answered yes to any of the aforementioned questions your personal productivity is likely not where it should be. Boosting personal productivity is virtually the only way for CEOs to meet their earnings expectations, keep their sanity by maintaining a balanced life and meet customer expectations.

Studies have shown that most CEOs, when objectively assessed, are found to view themselves as being more productive than they really are. This is even true with the classic over-achieving type "A" personalities. So, what separates the productive from the non-productive? In working with countless executives and entrepreneurs it has been my experience that those CEOs who like to cover a lot of ground and consider themselves masters of multi-tasking are not nearly as productive as those who have an ability to focus.

I am frequently asked what it takes to become more productive. My answer is simple…Become very, very focused. Focus has always been a characteristic that has served me well. In my life focus results in aligned priorities, order, discipline and productivity. Those things in turn result in balance and happiness. That sounds simple enough doesn't it? Then why is it so hard for CEOs to stay focused? Experience has shown me that there are two primary reasons that CEOs cannot maintain their focus:

1. Successful people tend to be energetic, creative, intelligent, and have bias toward action. That combination of personality traits combined with the pace at which business operates today can cause even the best and brightest to lose focus and in turn lose productivity, and;

2. They lack a programmatic, disciplined approach to maintaining their focus. Like most good things in life, focus doesn't usually happen by osmosis. It takes a systematic, process driven approach to maintain high levels of focus on a consistent long term basis.

I have seen many productivity systems over the years and for the most part they all have something good to offer. However the complaint that I have with most of them is that they are too complicated and they tend to look too far ahead. In the text that follows I will share with you the four-pronged strategy that I have used to maintain my focus for the last 20 years:

1. Vision: You must always have a clear vision of what is important to you and why you are doing what you're doing. It is this clarity of vision that dictates purpose and priority. If you don't know what you're playing for it is very difficult to compete much less to win.

2. Tactical Business Plans: I like to keep things to the short strokes. I work off rolling 90 day tactical business plans based upon achieving objectives that move me closer to the fulfillment of my vision. When you consistently string together quarter over quarter progress momentum is generated and great things happen.

3. Task Management: Every day for the last 20 years I have gone to work with an updated task list which contains 20 items that I want to try and accomplish that day. While I wish I could tell you that I'm able to accomplish all 20 items each day I can't. But what I can tell you is that those who know me will testify that I accomplish more in a day than many people will in a week or a month. The tasks are developed based upon achieving the 90 plan which is based upon fulfilling the overarching vision.

4. Gut Checks: This is the big one...Many people half-heartedly use task lists, but the key to consistently crossing items off the list is conducting hourly gut checks. Every hour on the hour I ask myself the following question. Am I doing the most productive thing possible at this point in time? If my answer is yes I press on. If my answer is no I have a decision to make...I have been known to end meetings, phone calls, recalendar appointments, etc. solely based on the outcome of my gut check. It is okay to spend time on items that don't meet the gut check test so long as you are aware that you're doing it. It is the people that think they're being productive when they are clearly not that have trouble.

This system has served me well for more than 20 years and I challenge you to put it to the test. I can guarantee you only one thing…If you don't try it you may never know the power that focus can bring to bear on your life.

Okay, let's examine an all too common scenario: You have 30 minutes before the beginning of a strategy meeting which you are facilitating, and as you start to prepare your final thoughts you receive an e-mail from legal asking you to review the latest version of an important contract before you go into the meeting. As you begin to redline the contract you receive an IM from the CFO asking for your immediate attention on a key issue. As you start to respond to the CFO your assistant informs you that an important client is on the phone and needs to speak with you immediately…As you begin to take the phone call you glance out your window only to see a small line forming outside your door, and just then your Blackberry goes-off with a 911 from your spouse…

The sad part about the aforementioned illustration is that for many CEOs this is standard operating procedure. The pressure to become a multi-tasking phenom is in my opinion at the root of a decline in executive productivity. Multi-tasking in my opinion is choosing to deal with perceived "urgent" matters rather than focusing on truly "important" matters. My father once told me that "part-time efforts yield part-time results" and I have found that with rare exception his premise is correct.

In the scenario presented above it is likely that this

fictional CEO would not have been properly prepared for his/her meeting, missed a key business point in reviewing the contract, sent the CFO an indiscernible IM full of typos, upset the important client by not giving the deserved amount of respect and attention, frustrated the co-workers lined-up outside the door and more than likely would have ended-up sleeping on the couch because he/she forgot to return their spouse's phone call.

It is impossible to kind-of, sort-of, almost focus and still be productive. If you find yourself constantly multi-tasking you are exhibiting a lack of focus, an inability to prioritize and regardless of what you might think, you are **not** optimizing your productivity. Rather than dance around issues CEOs need to hit issues head on by applying a laser-like focus and process to execution.

The problem with many CEOs is that they are actually addicted to the wrong types of activities. The first step in dealing with an addiction is to recognize it exists in the first place. Technology can be a beautiful thing but only if you learn to be its master and not its slave. Without question the most successful CEOs I know are the ones that can prioritize, delegate, focus and who understand the difference between a productive "no" and an unproductive "yes". Learning to stop trying to be all things to all people while attempting to single handedly conquer the world is what will help lead you toward a certainty of execution and an increase in productivity.

While we're on the topic of focus and productivity, I want to digress a moment and talk about one of my biggest pet-peeves...poorly orchestrated meetings. I'm afraid it is all too common that most meetings are not nearly as productive as they could be and sadly this is often times do to the fault of the CEO. Whether meetings are held at the board, executive, management or staff levels, or whether they are small project related meetings or large company-wide meetings, the same basic principles apply to making meetings effective.

Early in my career I worked for a company where the CEO loved to have meetings. Meetings were held ad-nauseum about virtually every topic under the sun. Regrettably these meetings rarely resulted in anything being accomplished, and in fact, because the meetings were poorly conceived and poorly facilitated it turned out that most meetings just ended-up being rehashing sessions for the subjects not resolved in prior meetings. Non productive meetings not only serve no purpose, but they waste one of the most precious resources that a company has...time. One of the biggest mistakes a CEO can make is to take top talent away from productive activities and sequester them away for a mind-numbing babble session. Bad meetings are not only a personal waste of time and productivity drain for the CEO, but they also can cause a decline in morale and a lack of confidence in leadership.

The reality is that there is no excuse to hold a non-productive meeting. I simply won't attend a meeting unless it is a good use of my time. You won't see my smiling face in attendance at a meeting unless I know why the meeting is being called, who's going to be in attendance, what the objectives (preferably hard deliverables) are for the meeting, and unless an agenda has been circulated in advance of the meeting allowing for proper preparation. Forget "Roberts Rules," following is a more detailed breakdown of Myatt's 10 rules for productive meetings:

1. **Culture**: As the CEO you need to create a culture where meetings are valued as a highest and best use activity and not a nuisance. If leadership doesn't value meetings then it will be impossible for the rest of the company to do so. At my firm an employee's contribution (or lack thereof)

to meetings is part of their formal performance review. People know that their contribution to meetings will not only have an impact on the company but on their paycheck as well. Meetings also need to be fun...I'm not talking about silly themes, or ice-breaking games, but rather having a relaxed, non-intimidating and professional atmosphere surrounding your meetings. If people know that they are valued, respected and won't be publicly embarrassed they will in turn be at ease and prepared to deliver.

2. **Calendaring**: Meetings need to have a start time and an end-time. If you can't accomplish the stated objectives within the time allotted then schedule a follow-up meeting to deal with unresolved items. Don't ask me to attend a meeting and then not start on time. In my firm there is a standing monetary fine imposed in 5 minute increments for tardiness...While this may sound harsh, I can tell you that it is extremely effective in that rarely is there such a thing as an attendee who is tardy. Also, try not to hold meetings during prime-time...I prefer meetings early in the morning, over lunch or at the end of the day. Don't take your team out of production during the meat of the day, rather take those times of the day that are typically the least productive times and hold your meetings then.

3. **Agenda**: I'm not a big fan of impromptu meetings. Creativity and innovation are stimulated by structure, not stifled by it. If the subject is worth addressing it is worth planning for and preparation takes time. A detailed agenda for a meeting should be circulated in advance to all attendees so that they have time to prepare to make a valuable contribution.

4. **Attendees**: Don't invite people to a meeting that have nothing to contribute and don't hold a meeting unless the key contributors can be in attendance. If a key person is not able to attend the meeting, reschedule for a time when

they can be in attendance. If you're coming to a meeting not prepared to make a valuable contribution why are you coming?

5. **Leadership**: Someone must be in charge of the meeting. All meetings should have a meeting chair responsible for keeping the meeting on point, on schedule and achieving the meeting objectives. Bad meetings are a result of bad leadership.

6. **Focus**: Cell phones and other PDA's need to be turned-off. Nothing can be accomplished when people are not giving 100% focused attention to the issue at hand. I can't tell you how many times I've attended meetings at client companies when more than half the attendees were sending e-mails and instant messages under the table while the meeting was in session. If a meeting is important enough to attend, it should demand the participant's full attention.

7. **Deliverables**: If the objectives of the meeting are not clearly articulated as a defined set of deliverables your meeting is not worth having. The purpose of a meeting is to accomplish something and you can't accomplish something if that something is vague, ambiguous, ethereal, or has not been defined to begin with.

8. **Technology**: Use technology to add value to your meetings. Use web conferencing to bring in contributors from other locations and to improve collaboration. Use audio or video to record your meetings so that no valuable piece of information falls through the cracks. If you can't use audio or video, then don't limit the value of a contributor by having them take minutes...call in an administrative person to fulfill that role. The proper use of technology can save time, increase efficiency and productivity and cut unnecessary travel expenses.

9. **Location**: Don't fall into the trap of going off-site

unless it is absolutely necessary. Off-site meetings are expensive not only in terms of the hard dollars spent on facilities, but also in terms of the commute time to and from the meeting. You should have the discipline to use your facilities in an uninterrupted fashion. Make it known that meetings are not to be interrupted unless it is an emergency (an "emergency" needs to be defined as both urgent and important).

10. **Assess and Evaluate**: The meeting chair should conduct a critical post-meeting analyses to determine what went well, what went wrong, were the right people in attendance, were the people prepared, were the deliverables met, etc. The bottom line is that companies that have great meetings have great meetings for a reason...they work on it.

Chapter 9

The Traps that Great CEOs Avoid

"Landmines are everywhere in business, but the great
CEO knows where he can walk confidently, where he
must tread softly, and where he must never go at all."
— Mike Myatt

Your ability to have long term success as a CEO is
just as much about avoiding critical mistakes as it
is about how accomplished you are. Your ledger of
accomplishments can be 10 miles long, but all it takes is
one mistake to watch everything evaporate right in front of
your eyes (recall the earlier discussion on decisioning). In
this chapter I'll highlight some of the most common traps
to avoid if you want to thrive as a CEO…

Best Practices: Even though I will from time-to-time
slip and refer to something as "Best Practices" I am
attempting to extricate that phrase from my vocabulary. I
have actually come to cringe every time I hear a so called
expert use the phrase in an authoritarian manner as a

justification for the position they happen to be evangelizing. In the brief text that follows I will put forth my perspectives on this subject which are meant to reveal the many hidden dangers that are often associated with Best Practices implementations...

Let me begin with a bold statement that I'm sure will unleash the wrath of many: "There is no such thing as best practices" and you can feel free to quote me on that...Best Practices are nothing more than disparate groups of methodologies, processes, rules, concepts and theories that have had success in certain areas, and because of those successes, have been deemed as universal truths that can be applied anywhere and everywhere resulting in dramatic improvements. Just because someone says something doesn't mean it's true...Moreover just because company A had success with a certain initiative doesn't mean that company B can plug-and-play the same process and expect the same outcome. As a CEO you must not rely on generic canned solutions as a cure-all, for if you do, your organization will suffer tremendously.

Let's use an example of a common problem that most businesses face at some point in their lifecycle (if not at multiple points) which is needing to implement a certain application or toolset to automate an existing manual process. Okay, my question is this: What constitutes best practices in this situation? Does the company purchase an off-the-shelf solution, utilize an ASP (Application Service Provider) solution or embark upon developing a custom application? Moreover if they decide to develop the application should this be done internally with existing staff, or outsourced, and if outsourced will it be done domestically or offshore and who will manage the process. Oh, and what about development methodology? I could go on ad-nauseum with this line of thinking, but I'm sure you get the point by now. The reality is that you can find someone who will tell you that anyone of the options mentioned above constitutes best practices, so who is right and who is wrong?

It has been my experience that whenever methodologies become productized objectivity is removed from the equation. Whenever you are being pitched a product as a solution I suggest you exercise extreme caution. Business is fluid, dynamic and ever evolving, which means that static advice at best is short lived, but most times is simply incongruous with the very nature of business itself. I'm not looking for someone to cram my enterprise into their set of canned rules and processes, rather I'm looking for someone to tailor a solution based upon the unique circumstances of my environment.

My experience has been consistent over the years in that whenever a common aspect of business turns into a "practice area" and the heard mentality of the politically correct legions of consultants and advisors use said area as a platform to be evangelized, the necessity of common sense and the reality of what actually works often times gets thrown out the window as a trade-off for promotional gain. It is precisely the dispensing of one-size fits all advice that has allowed the ranks of consultants and other professional advisors to swell to historical proportions. After all, if you can apply someone else's theory in a vacuum it lowers the barrier to entry doesn't it? Labeling something as Best Practices is not a substitute for wisdom, discernment, discretion, subject matter expertise, intellect, creativity or any of the other qualities I value in an advisor.

Popular business axioms and management theories are thrown around in such cavalier fashion these days that they can actually result in flawed decisioning. It is for precisely this reason that I believe too much common management wisdom is not wise at all, but instead flawed knowledge based on a misunderstanding or misapplication of "best practices" that often constitutes poor, incomplete or outright obsolete thinking.

Let's look at this from another angle...As a CEO, why would you want to do business in the same fashion as your competitors? Don't utilize your competition's practices, but rather innovate around them and improve upon them to create an advantage that can be leveraged in the market. Reflect back to the chapter on innovation and become disruptive in your approach. Do not fall into the trap of doing something in a particular fashion just because others do it that way...

Bottom line...Just because a professor says it's so, a consultant recommends it, a book has been written on it, or a product has been developed for it doesn't mean that whatever "it" is constitutes the right option for you. I have personally witnessed companies that embarked upon an enterprise-wide initiative because they were sold on "best practices". After two years into a seven-figure implementation, without any meaningful benefit, they woke-up to the fact that purchasing a product as a solution rarely constitutes best practices.

Key Employees: I have rarely come across a CEO who hasn't struggled with the issue of dealing with key employees, and the truth is that most CEOs handle this issue improperly. While much has been written on the subject of hiring and retaining key employees, in my opinion most of it flat misses the mark. In fact, I'll go so far to say that key employees are not assets but rather large contingent liabilities. If you have stooped to the level of paying hiring or retention bonuses or find yourself otherwise being held hostage by those employees who feel like they are indispensable you are only exacerbating the problem. I'm not disputing the need to hire or retain talent but I am vehemently disputing the conventional wisdom of how most businesses address the risk of managing key employees. Let me offer you some relief and give you a fresh perspective on the age old dilemma of how to deal with key employees...

As a CEO your problem with key employees begins the very second you publicly identify someone as such. The fact that you have a key employee to begin with means that at a minimum you have a lack of transparency and continuity in your organization and more probably that you lack depth of talent and are weak in process and knowledge management. The truth of the matter is that all employees are key employees...they have a role to play and their contributions are important. As the CEO you must learn to motivate and reward someone without elevating them to a stature that creates potential operational, philosophical and emotional problems for your organization.

How would you answer this question...Is your company talent poor and key employee dependant, or talent rich or key employee independent? In my world a superstar is not necessarily the same thing as a key employee...There is a monumental difference between real tier-one talent and a primadonna who thinks of themselves as tier-one talent. Employees who represent true tier-one talent see themselves as part of the team seeking to make those around them more successful. Contrast this with those primadonnas who are interested solely in their own success without regard to those around them. Any company that bestows a primadonna with recognition as a key employee is a company about ready to experience a completely avoidable disaster.

Over the years I have learned that no one and I mean no one is indispensable. A well managed company is not dependant upon the performance of any single individual. Those individuals who attempt to hoard knowledge, relationships or resources to attain job security are not to be valued as key, but are to be admonished as ineffective and deemed a liability. Corporate talent that cannot be shared, duplicated, distributed or leveraged is not nearly as valuable as talent that can (refer back to the section on knowledge management).

If you want to eliminate dependency on key employees don't allow any individual to create ultimate domain over anything that is considered key or mission critical. Instead create a culture that values transparency, knowledge management, mentoring, coaching and process. By doing these things you will add both depth and breadth to your organization and increase the overall level of talent across the enterprise.

Trend Following: Does your business exploit trends or do they exploit your business? What was the latest fad chased or trend adopted by your business? As the CEO, why did you jump on the band wagon? Has the trend or fad generated an increase in revenue or gains in efficiency and/or productivity? Let's examine the impact trends can have on your business.

I want to begin by pointing out that trends and fads don't necessarily constitute innovation. The truth is that the organizations that demonstrate a "herd mentality" when rushing to adopt the latest trends are the farthest thing from being innovative companies. The result is that they will likely experience little more than yet another in a long line of great adventures that ended in frustration due to the time wasted and the investment squandered. The reality is that many businesses are quick to recognize great ideas, but they often have no plan for how to successfully integrate them into their business model.

My advice to you is not to let your business get caught up in trends and fads...At least not without some initial analysis being conducted to determine the likelihood of success. Failed initiatives are costly at several levels. Aside from being costly, a flawed execution can cast doubt on your credibility, have a negative impact on morale, taint both your personal and corporate brand, adversely affect external relationships and cause a variety of other problematic issues for your enterprise.

Every sound business initiative should have a solid strategic plan. However while most anyone can coble together a high level strategic plan, very few can author a strategy that can be successfully implemented. In order for your enterprise to turn a trend or fad into a monetizing and/or value creating event you should develop a strategic plan that attempts to assess the idea against the following 15 elements:

1. The trend or fad should be in alignment with the overall vision and mission of the enterprise.

2. If the initiative doesn't provide a unique competitive advantage it should at least bring you closer to an even playing field.

3. Any new project should preferably add value to existing initiatives, and if not, it should show a significant enough return on investment to justify the dilutive effect of not keeping the main thing the main thing.

4. Put the idea through a risk/reward and cost/benefit analysis.

5. Whether the new initiative is intended for your organization, vendors, suppliers, partners or customers it must easy to use. Usability drives adoptability, and therefore it pays to keep things simple.

6. Just because an idea sounds good doesn't mean it is…You should endeavor to validate proof of concept based upon detailed, credible research.

7. Nothing is without risk, and when you think something is without risk that is when you're most likely to end-up in trouble. All initiatives should include detailed risk management provisions.

8. Adopting a trend or fad should be based upon solid business logic that drives corresponding financial engineering and modeling. Be careful of high level, pie-in-the-sky projections.

9. Any new initiative should contain accountability provisions. Every task should be assigned and managed according to a plan and in the light of day.

10. Any trend being adopted must be measurable. Deliverables, benchmarks, deadlines, and success metrics must be incorporated into the plan.

11. It must be detailed and deliverable on a schedule. The initiative should have a beginning, middle and end.

12. Strategic initiatives must not be disparate systems, but integrated solutions that eliminate redundancies, and build in tactical leverage points.

13. It must contain a roadmap for versioning and evolution that is in alignment with other strategic initiatives and the overall corporate mission.

14. A successful initiative cannot remain in a strategic planning state. It must be actionable through tactical implementation.

15. Great CEOs must champion any new initiative. Also be aware that if someone else at the C-suite level is against the new initiative it may likely die on the cutting-room floor.

The bottom line is that new ideas are beautiful things. Properly implemented, capitalizing on trends can keep business from stagnating and cause growth and evolution. Don't allow trends to cannibalize your business, rather just follow the 15 rules noted above and stay away from being an agent for change for the sake of change.

Accountability: Regardless of where you are in the corporate hierarchy, accountability is a fundamental principle associated with success. Administrative and support staff needs to be accountable for the quality and timeliness of their work. Sales people need to be accountable for not only production volume, but the manner in which they represent the company brand while attaining said volume. Management needs to be accountable to their subordinates as well as to executive leadership. Executives need to be accountable for their quality of leadership and decision making. As logical as all this seems it is rarely deemed a priority. It is in fact a lack of accountability that is the eventual undoing of many CEOs. As a CEO you cannot operate with the mentality that you are above everyone else and therefore the rules don't apply to you...Rather you must see yourself as being the most accountable person in the organization having the greatest burden for representing the best interests of others.

Accountability is the lowest cost, most practical and most productive form of risk management and quality assurance that can be implemented across an enterprise. It is really nothing more than a common sense understanding that decisions made within a framework are going to have a greater chance of success than those made in a vacuum.

It is those CEOs who don't believe they are accountable to anyone for anything at anytime that are nothing more than a disaster waiting to happen. All human beings regardless of who they are can be capable of making huge mistakes when operating in a vacuum or under a veil of secrecy. While there are certainly those individuals who are just predatory, bad to the bone people, clearly not everyone who makes a mistake is evil with the intent to do harm to others. Rather some CEOs when faced with a tough situation, and who find themselves not operating in an environment of accountability, will simply end-up making a regrettable decision that they would not have otherwise made if they were openly operating under the scrutiny and review of others.

If you think back to any of the bad and/or regrettable decisions you've made in your life it is highly probable that you didn't seek the counsel of others (or ignored said counsel) prior to making the wrong decision. Setting up an enterprise wide framework for accountability is as simple as implementing the following three items:

1. Have a clearly articulated statement of corporate values: Not only state the values that you want the entity to use as a foundation for operation, but also use the values to frame your vision, mission, strategy, tactics and processes. Hire and manage based upon the corporate values. If you hire someone who doesn't share the corporate values or don't hold existing employees accountable for maintaining the corporate values then you will get what you deserve...

2. Have a written delegation of authority: A written guideline for corporate decisioning will help individuals make good decisions. Describe in great detail which employees are authorized to make what decisions. Establish budgetary and approval guidelines for all decisions.

Making sure that good checks and balances are in place will help keep employees accountable. Don't fall into the trap of turning a blind eye and being reckless under the guise of "empowering" your employees, rather hold them accountable and you'll be rewarded with their respect.

3. Implement a good leadership development program: Utilizing training, coaching, mentoring, peer review, talent management and other development practices will help insure that your leaders will continue to grow and that corporate accountability guidelines are being consistently reinforced. The bottom line is that every individual in your organization can become more productive and satisfied as a result of coaching, mentoring or other forms of leadership development programs.

Politically Correct Thinking. There are few things in business and in life in general that I loathe more than those who adopt a politically correct stance. As a CEO you cannot fall into the trap of confusing what is fair and right with being politically correct as they are radically different concepts. In my opinion politically correct thinking is a large contributor to a decrease in workplace productivity, and of greater concern, to the moral and ethical decay of our society. Are these extreme statements? Perhaps some may think so, but being authentic to my politically incorrect self, I think not.

Before those of dissenting (politically correct) opinions become too outraged with my position let me be perfectly clear that I believe strongly in fairness, respect and tolerance. These characteristics should be present in all human beings and are admirable qualities so long as they don't take precedence over, ignore or contradict truth. The problem with politically correct thinking is that it confuses kindness and courtesy with bureaucratic mandates and strips people of their real opinions. Politically correct thinking replaces individuality and authentic opinions with socially acceptable rhetoric and watered-down behavioral tendencies. I actually miss the days when most conversations consisted of unpredictable, highly charged and stimulating discourse where people were encouraged to openly share their true thoughts and opinions.

The irony of politically correct thinking is that a society void of individual thought actually creates the opposite of diversity…it is this type of thinking that results in a brainwashed group of sheep who completely lack diversity as a result of a generification of thoughts and actions. The dark secret behind politically correct thinking is that it slowly dulls your senses and neuters your innate ability to be discerning. I don't know about you, but I don't want to hear what you think I want you to say, or what you think you should say, but rather I want to hear what you're really thinking. Have you ever sat in a meeting where all parties sit around the table with a deer in the headlights look trying to figure out how to dance around an issue rather than address it head-on? It is this type of invisible elephant in the room that can pollute your corporate culture by stifling innovation and undermining productivity. Those CEOs who embrace politically correct thinking sentence themselves to a culture of mediocrity.

The issues of safety and security also come into play when dealing with politically correct thinking. The sad reality is that many people believe so strongly that there is safety in numbers that they will compromise their own thoughts and ultimately their integrity by adopting a safe position rather than take the risk of standing strongly for their beliefs. It has become more important to "do things right" rather than to "do the right things." Blending-in has become in vogue while making waves via independent thinking has become socially inappropriate behavior.

Wouldn't it be more prudent to let the facts and/or truth surrounding a particular matter rise above the rhetoric and guide your actions rather than to blindly adopt an attitude of political correctness? Of course it would, except for one huge problem...in the face of conflict, dissention, threats or controversy, people tend to turn to the mind's medicine cabinet and take a few denial, justification and rationalization pills. In today's politically correct world it is easier to hide in the safety of the majority and coast along without making any waves than it is to take on the risk of being outspoken, innovative, disruptive, challenging, convicted, bold or controversial...Therein lies the problem with political correctness.

Great CEOs create an environment where respect is required, excellence is demanded and politically correct behavior is not tolerated. Make waves and challenge the status quo...don't succumb to it.

Postscript
It's How You Finish that Counts

"We rate the ability in men by what they finish, not by what they attempt"

- Unknown

Anyone who has ever run a race can attest to the fact that the most difficult, yet important part of any race is what occurs down the home stretch as you near the finish line. This is not only where the training and preparation really pays off, but it is also where the runner who can reach down and draw upon a will to win can sometimes steal the victory from other runners with less intestinal fortitude.

As I mentioned in the introduction of this book, it is important to build your career in such a fashion that you don't reach the finish line emotionally bankrupt, unfulfilled, and with a plethora of broken relationships left in your wake. The reason that I chose to present these thoughts in a postscript as opposed to using an entire chapter is that I don't want to lose you here. While I'm going to climb-up on my soap box one last time, I promise to keep it brief. All I ask is that you give the following thoughts serious consideration, and if you do I can promise you that you'll be happy you did.

By the time you reach the CEO level you should be striving to move beyond success and toward significance. You need to use your network, your wealth, your experience and intellect as well as your passion to create a legacy that transcends your title. My wife has always said to place your investments into those who will be crying at your funeral. If you think back on your career and look at all the investments made into people and things that really don't matter you'll find that you've squandered many valuable resources. Let me be clear here…I believe all people matter within the context that everyone is a human being. However it is the types of investments you make and the reasoning behind those investments that I'm asking you to assess.

If it seems trite to be asking you to ponder if you are in fact leaving things better than you found them then I would suggest that you reconsider your values and your vision. As a CEO you have the ability to influence positive changes and to make contributions well beyond those who have not been afforded the same opportunities, and it would be nothing short of tragic for you not to clearly understand this. While it is never too late to begin thinking about finishing well, the simple truth of the matter is that the longer you wait to begin thinking on a significant level the less significant your legacy will be.

In previous chapters we discussed at great length the benefit of personal branding and the concept of sustainability. However I want you now to consider those concepts as they relate to your legacy…Do your career minded decisions reconcile with your legacy minded goals? Now that you've finished this book and absorbed all the material I want you to go back and re-read the fist chapter as it relates to this postscript and update your original gut-check to see if anything has changed.

Best wishes for continued success...

Breinigsville, PA USA
11 August 2010
243413BV00002B/16/A